PyTorch LLM

Train, Fine-Tune, and Deploy Large Language Models for Real-World Applications

Charles Sprinter

Disclaimer
The information in this book is provided "as is," with no guarantees of
completeness, or fitness for any particular purpose. The author and
publisher do not accept any responsibility for errors or omissions, or for
any outcomes arising from the use of the material contained in this book.

Trademarks
PyTorch is a trademark of Facebook, Inc.
Other brand and product names are trademarks or registered
trademarks of their respective companies.

Table of Contents

Preface

Welcome to **"PyTorch LLM: Train, Fine-Tune, and Deploy Large Language Models for Real-World Applications"**! This book is designed to equip you with the knowledge and tools needed to master PyTorch and leverage it for developing cutting-edge Large Language Models (LLMs). Whether you are a beginner taking your first steps into the world of deep learning or a seasoned professional looking to expand your expertise, this book has something for everyone.

1.1 Why PyTorch and LLMs Are Transforming AI

Artificial Intelligence (AI) has experienced exponential growth in recent years, with applications spanning industries such as healthcare, finance, education, and entertainment. Among the numerous AI tools and frameworks available, **PyTorch** and **Large Language Models (LLMs)** have emerged as two pivotal technologies driving innovation.

Why PyTorch?

PyTorch is one of the most popular frameworks for developing and deploying deep learning models. Its advantages include:

- **Ease of Use**: PyTorch's intuitive syntax and dynamic computation graph make it a favorite among developers and researchers.
- **Flexibility**: Ideal for prototyping, PyTorch allows developers to experiment with model architectures easily.
- **Scalability**: With support for distributed training, PyTorch is well-suited for handling large-scale models.
- **Strong Community**: A vast and active community ensures access to resources, tutorials, and libraries.

Why LLMs?

Large Language Models, such as GPT, BERT, and T5, represent a significant leap in natural language processing (NLP). Their ability to understand, generate, and manipulate human language has revolutionized fields like:

- **Customer Support**: Building chatbots and virtual assistants.
- **Healthcare**: Assisting in diagnostics and summarizing medical literature.

- **Finance**: Summarizing documents and identifying trends.
- **Education**: Personalizing learning experiences and automating content generation.

Together, PyTorch and LLMs provide a powerful combination for solving real-world problems, making them essential tools for AI practitioners.

1.2 Who This Book Is For

This book is designed to cater to a diverse audience, including:

1. **Beginners**:
   - If you are new to PyTorch or machine learning, this book provides step-by-step instructions, clear explanations, and hands-on exercises to build your skills from the ground up.
2. **Researchers**:
   - For those exploring new frontiers in AI, this book dives into advanced topics like distributed training, optimization techniques, and transformer architectures.
3. **Engineers**:
   - Software engineers and data scientists looking to deploy AI solutions will find practical guidance on deploying LLMs in real-world applications.
4. **Industry Professionals**:
   - If you're working in industries like healthcare, finance, or education, this book demonstrates how to adapt and fine-tune LLMs for domain-specific tasks.

1.3 How to Use This Book

To maximize your learning experience, this book has been structured to combine theory with hands-on practice. Here's how to navigate the content effectively:

Interactive Notebooks
- Throughout the book, you'll find links to **interactive Jupyter notebooks** and **Google Colab environments** where you can run the code examples directly.

Step-by-Step Progression
- The chapters are arranged to build upon one another:
  - Start with the basics of PyTorch and LLMs.

- Gradually move into advanced topics like distributed training, optimization, and deployment.
- Apply your knowledge in real-world projects at the end of each section.

Code and Troubleshooting
- All code snippets are tested for accuracy and include comments explaining each step.
- Troubleshooting tips are provided to help you resolve common errors.

Projects and Exercises
- Every chapter includes a hands-on project or exercise to reinforce learning.
- These projects are designed to be practical and relevant to real-world applications.

1.4 Overview of Key Features and Hands-On Projects

This book emphasizes learning through doing. Below is an overview of key features and projects:

Key Features
- **High-Quality Code Examples**:
  - All code examples are clean, well-documented, and optimized for clarity and performance.
- **Real-World Applications**:
  - Learn to build chatbots, summarize documents, and deploy models in production environments.
- **Advanced Topics**:
  - Explore distributed training, optimization techniques, and the latest trends in LLMs.
- **Visual Aids**:
  - Diagrams and flowcharts simplify complex concepts.

Sample Hands-On Projects
- **Train a Small Transformer from Scratch**:
  - Build and train a basic transformer model for text generation.
- **Fine-Tune a Pre-Trained GPT Model**:
  - Adapt GPT for a custom chatbot application.
- **Deploy a Question-Answering API**:
  - Use FastAPI to deploy a fine-tuned model on the cloud.

These projects will not only reinforce your understanding but also provide you with a portfolio of work that you can showcase.

1.5 Companion Resources

To enhance your learning experience, this book is supported by a variety of companion resources:

Code Repositories

- A GitHub repository accompanies this book, containing:
    - All code examples.
    - Pre-trained models.
    - Datasets used in exercises.

Community Forums

- Join our online community to:
    - Discuss projects and solutions with fellow readers.
    - Get support for troubleshooting issues.
    - Stay updated on the latest PyTorch and LLM developments.

This book is your gateway to mastering PyTorch and Large Language Models, equipping you with the skills to tackle real-world AI challenges. Whether you're building your first chatbot or scaling billion-parameter models, this book will guide you every step of the way.

Let's embark on this exciting journey into the world of PyTorch and LLMs!

Chapter 1: Understanding AI Workflows and Large Language Models

In this chapter, we will explore the foundations of Large Language Models (LLMs), their role in modern AI workflows, and why PyTorch is a preferred framework for their development. You'll also gain insights into how LLMs compare to other frameworks and their applications across industries.

1.1 What Are Large Language Models (LLMs)?

Large Language Models (LLMs) are advanced artificial intelligence models designed to understand, generate, and manipulate human language. These models are built using billions of parameters and trained on massive datasets to achieve remarkable capabilities in natural language processing (NLP) tasks.

Key Characteristics of LLMs:
- **Scale**: LLMs, like GPT-3, have billions of parameters, allowing them to capture complex linguistic patterns.
- **Versatility**: They can perform diverse tasks, such as text generation, translation, summarization, and question answering.
- **Pre-Training and Fine-Tuning**: Most LLMs are first pre-trained on large datasets and then fine-tuned for specific tasks.
- **Transformer-Based Architecture**: LLMs rely on the transformer architecture, which uses attention mechanisms to process input sequences efficiently.

Examples of Popular LLMs:

Model	Organization	Capabilities
GPT-3	OpenAI	Text generation, chatbots, and more
BERT	Google	Text classification, NER, Q&A
T5	Google	Text-to-text generation tasks
LLaMA	Meta AI	Lightweight and efficient LLM

1.2 Common AI Workflows in NLP and Beyond

AI workflows in NLP involve a series of steps to prepare data, train models, and deploy solutions. These workflows can vary based on the complexity of the task but generally follow these stages:

1. Data Collection and Preparation

- Collect raw text data from sources like web pages, documents, or APIs.
- Clean and preprocess the data:
    - Remove unnecessary characters or duplicates.
    - Tokenize the text into smaller units (words, subwords, or characters).

Example Code for Tokenization:

python

```python
from transformers import AutoTokenizer

# Load a tokenizer
tokenizer = AutoTokenizer.from_pretrained("bert-base-uncased")

# Tokenize sample text
text = "PyTorch makes LLMs easier to develop."
tokens = tokenizer.tokenize(text)
print("Tokens:", tokens)
```

2. Model Training

- Use pre-trained models or train from scratch on specific datasets.
- Implement optimizers, schedulers, and loss functions to improve model performance.

Training Workflow Example:

1. Load the data.
2. Build the model using a transformer architecture.
3. Train the model with batches of tokenized data.
4. Validate and fine-tune for the target task.

3. Evaluation

- Evaluate the model using metrics like accuracy, BLEU score (for translation), or F1 score (for classification).

4. Deployment
- Deploy the trained model as a web service or API using frameworks like FastAPI or TorchServe.

Deployment Code Example:

python

```python
from fastapi import FastAPI
from transformers import
AutoModelForSequenceClassification, AutoTokenizer

app = FastAPI()

# Load model and tokenizer
model =
AutoModelForSequenceClassification.from_pretrained("b
ert-base-uncased")
tokenizer = AutoTokenizer.from_pretrained("bert-base-
uncased")

@app.post("/predict")
def predict(text: str):
    inputs = tokenizer(text, return_tensors="pt")
    outputs = model(**inputs)
    return {"prediction": outputs.logits.argmax(-
1).item()}
```

1.3 Why Choose PyTorch for LLM Development?

PyTorch has become the go-to framework for developing Large Language Models due to its flexibility, ease of use, and strong community support.

Key Advantages of PyTorch:
1. **Dynamic Computation Graphs**:
   - PyTorch builds the computation graph dynamically, making debugging and experimentation easier.
2. **Ease of Prototyping**:

- o Its Pythonic nature allows researchers to quickly implement and test new ideas.

3. **Scalability**:
   - o PyTorch supports distributed training, enabling developers to train large models across multiple GPUs or nodes.

4. **Rich Ecosystem**:
   - o Integration with libraries like Hugging Face Transformers simplifies the process of fine-tuning LLMs.

Code Example: Simple PyTorch Training Loop

python

```python
import torch
import torch.nn as nn
import torch.optim as optim

# Define a simple model
model = nn.Linear(10, 1)

# Loss function and optimizer
criterion = nn.MSELoss()
optimizer = optim.SGD(model.parameters(), lr=0.01)

# Training loop
for epoch in range(5):
    inputs = torch.randn(32, 10)
    targets = torch.randn(32, 1)

    # Forward pass
    outputs = model(inputs)
    loss = criterion(outputs, targets)

    # Backward pass and optimization
    optimizer.zero_grad()
    loss.backward()
    optimizer.step()

    print(f"Epoch [{epoch+1}/5], Loss:
{loss.item():.4f}")
```

1.4 Comparing PyTorch with TensorFlow and JAX

While PyTorch is widely popular, TensorFlow and JAX are also significant frameworks for deep learning and LLM development. Here's how they compare:

Feature	PyTorch	TensorFlow	JAX
Ease of Use	Intuitive and Pythonic	Steeper learning curve	Focused on researchers
Debugging	Dynamic computation graph	Static computation graph	Designed for speed
Ecosystem	Hugging Face, Lightning	TensorFlow Hub	Flax, Optax
Distributed Training	Excellent support	Good support	Best for research
Adoption	Research and industry	Industry-focused	Research-specific

1.5 Real-World Use Cases for LLMs Across Industries

Large Language Models have transformed numerous industries by enabling advanced NLP capabilities. Below are some notable applications:

1. Healthcare

- **Clinical Trial Matching**: Analyze patient records to recommend suitable trials.
- **Medical Literature Summarization**: Summarize long research papers for quick reference.

2. Finance

- **Fraud Detection**: Analyze transaction patterns and flag anomalies.

- **Document Summarization**: Automatically condense financial reports.

3. Education
- **Personalized Learning**: Create customized content for students based on their needs.
- **Automated Grading**: Evaluate student essays using LLMs.

4. Customer Support
- **Chatbots**: Develop virtual assistants for handling customer queries.
- **Sentiment Analysis**: Understand customer feedback for better decision-making.

This chapter has introduced the foundational concepts of LLMs, common AI workflows, and the advantages of using PyTorch. It also highlighted the growing role of LLMs across industries, showcasing their transformative impact. As we progress, you'll gain hands-on experience with these concepts to build, fine-tune, and deploy your own LLMs.

Sample Code: Comparing PyTorch and TensorFlow for a Simple Neural Network

In this section, we'll compare PyTorch and TensorFlow by implementing a simple feedforward neural network in both frameworks. The goal is to highlight the usability differences, such as code structure, syntax, and debugging capabilities.

Scenario:
We will build a neural network with:
1. **Input Layer**: 10 features.
2. **Hidden Layer**: 20 neurons with ReLU activation.
3. **Output Layer**: 1 output neuron for regression.
4. **Task**: Train the network on random data for 5 epochs.

PyTorch Implementation
Step-by-Step Explanation
1. **Define the Model**: Use torch.nn.Module to build the network.

2. **Define Loss and Optimizer**: Use Mean Squared Error (MSE) as the loss function and Stochastic Gradient Descent (SGD) as the optimizer.
3. **Training Loop**: Iterate over multiple epochs, compute the loss, and update the weights.

Code

python

```python
import torch
import torch.nn as nn
import torch.optim as optim

# Define the model
class SimpleNN(nn.Module):
    def __init__(self):
        super(SimpleNN, self).__init__()
        self.fc1 = nn.Linear(10, 20)  # Input to
Hidden Layer
        self.relu = nn.ReLU()         # Activation
Function
        self.fc2 = nn.Linear(20, 1)  # Hidden to
Output Layer

    def forward(self, x):
        x = self.fc1(x)
        x = self.relu(x)
        x = self.fc2(x)
        return x

# Initialize the model, loss function, and optimizer
model = SimpleNN()
criterion = nn.MSELoss()  # Mean Squared Error Loss
optimizer = optim.SGD(model.parameters(), lr=0.01)

# Training Loop
for epoch in range(5):
    # Generate random data
    inputs = torch.randn(32, 10)  # Batch of 32
samples, 10 features each
```

```
    targets = torch.randn(32, 1)   # Batch of 32
target values

    # Forward pass
    outputs = model(inputs)
    loss = criterion(outputs, targets)

    # Backward pass and optimization
    optimizer.zero_grad()
    loss.backward()
    optimizer.step()

    print(f"Epoch [{epoch+1}/5], Loss:
{loss.item():.4f}")
```

TensorFlow Implementation
Step-by-Step Explanation
1. **Define the Model**: Use TensorFlow's tf.keras.Sequential to build the network.
2. **Compile the Model**: Specify the loss function (MSE) and optimizer (SGD) in the compile method.
3. **Training Loop**: Use fit to train the model for the specified number of epochs.

Code
python

```
import tensorflow as tf
from tensorflow.keras import Sequential
from tensorflow.keras.layers import Dense
from tensorflow.keras.optimizers import SGD

# Define the model
model = Sequential([
    Dense(20, activation='relu', input_shape=(10,)),
# Input to Hidden Layer
    Dense(1)
# Hidden to Output Layer
])
```

18

```
# Compile the model
model.compile(optimizer=SGD(learning_rate=0.01),
loss='mse')

# Generate random data
inputs = tf.random.normal((32, 10))  # Batch of 32
samples, 10 features each
targets = tf.random.normal((32, 1))  # Batch of 32
target values

# Train the model
history = model.fit(inputs, targets, epochs=5,
verbose=1)
```

Comparison Table: PyTorch vs. TensorFlow

Feature	PyTorch	TensorFlow
Model Definition	Explicitly define layers using torch.nn.Module.	Use Sequential for simplicity or subclassing.
Training Loop	Requires a custom loop for forward/backward passes.	Automated with the fit method.
Loss Function	Explicitly compute loss during the loop.	Defined in the compile method.
Optimizer	Manually update gradients with zero_grad and step.	Automatically handled within fit.
Flexibility	High (custom loops allow more control).	Moderate (simplifies common tasks).

Key Observations
PyTorch:
- Offers greater control over the training process with explicit forward/backward passes and gradient updates.
- Best suited for researchers and developers who need flexibility for experimentation and debugging.

TensorFlow:
- Automates many aspects of training, such as forward/backward passes and gradient updates, making it easier for beginners and production scenarios.

- Simplified workflows may limit flexibility for custom operations.

Both PyTorch and TensorFlow have their strengths and weaknesses. PyTorch's dynamic computation graph provides flexibility and ease of debugging, while TensorFlow's automation simplifies standard workflows. Your choice should depend on the requirements of your project—PyTorch for research and experimentation, and TensorFlow for production-grade pipelines.

Chapter 2: Setting Up for Success

To effectively work with PyTorch and Large Language Models (LLMs), setting up your development environment is crucial. This chapter will guide you through the installation and configuration of PyTorch, Hugging Face Transformers, PyTorch Lightning, and tools like Jupyter Notebooks. We'll also cover advanced configurations such as CUDA for GPU acceleration, multi-GPU setups, and cloud environments, ensuring a smooth workflow.

2.1 Installing PyTorch for CPU and GPU Configurations

PyTorch provides flexibility by supporting both CPU and GPU installations. To ensure optimal performance, especially for large models, GPU acceleration is highly recommended.

Step 1: Check System Compatibility
Before installation, verify:
- Your Python version (PyTorch supports Python 3.7+).
- Your operating system (Linux, Windows, or macOS).
- GPU compatibility (CUDA version must match your GPU drivers).

Step 2: Install PyTorch
PyTorch offers an installation command generator on its official website. Below are sample commands:
For CPU Installation:
bash

```
pip install torch torchvision torchaudio
```
For GPU Installation:
　　1.　Check your CUDA version:
bash

```
nvcc --version
```
Example output:
yaml

CUDA Version: 11.8
    2. Use the appropriate command:
bash

```
pip install torch torchvision torchaudio --index-url
https://download.pytorch.org/whl/cu118
```

Verification Code: After installation, verify PyTorch:
python

```
import torch

# Check PyTorch version
print("PyTorch version:", torch.__version__)

# Check GPU availability
device = torch.device("cuda" if
torch.cuda.is_available() else "cpu")
print("Device:", device)
```

2.2 Setting Up Hugging Face Transformers, Datasets, and PyTorch Lightning

Installing Hugging Face Libraries
Hugging Face provides tools for working with pre-trained models and datasets.
    1. Install transformers and datasets:
bash

```
pip install transformers datasets
```

    2. Verify installation:
python

```
from transformers import pipeline

# Load a sentiment analysis pipeline
sentiment_analyzer = pipeline("sentiment-analysis")
```

```
result = sentiment_analyzer("PyTorch makes LLMs
easy!")
print(result)
```

Installing PyTorch Lightning

PyTorch Lightning simplifies training loops and supports advanced features like distributed training.

1. Install Lightning:

bash

pip install pytorch-lightning

2. Verify installation:

python

```
from pytorch_lightning import Trainer
print("PyTorch Lightning is installed and ready to
use.")
```

2.3 Configuring Jupyter Notebooks and IDEs for Seamless Coding

Installing Jupyter Notebooks

Jupyter is an interactive environment for coding and visualization.

1. Install Jupyter:

bash

pip install notebook

2. Launch Jupyter:

bash

jupyter notebook

3. Create a new Python 3 notebook and test:

python

```
print("Jupyter Notebook is working!")
```

Setting Up VS Code

Visual Studio Code (VS Code) is a powerful IDE for Python development.

1. Download and install VS Code from here.
2. Install the Python extension:
   - Open VS Code.

- o Go to Extensions (Ctrl+Shift+X or Cmd+Shift+X) and search for "Python".
- o Install the "Python" extension by Microsoft.
3. Configure the Python interpreter:
- o Press Ctrl+Shift+P and select "Python: Select Interpreter".
- o Choose the environment where PyTorch is installed.

Code Example in VS Code:
python

```
import torch
print("PyTorch in VS Code:", torch.__version__)
```

2.4 Working with CUDA, Multi-GPU, and Cloud Environments
Using CUDA for GPU Acceleration
1. Ensure CUDA is installed:
bash

```
nvcc --version
```

2. Install PyTorch with the correct CUDA version (as shown in **2.1**).
Multi-GPU Training
PyTorch supports multi-GPU training via torch.nn.DataParallel.
Example Code for Multi-GPU Training:
python

```
import torch
import torch.nn as nn

# Define a simple model
model = nn.Linear(10, 1)

# Wrap the model for multi-GPU
if torch.cuda.device_count() > 1:
    print(f"Using {torch.cuda.device_count()} GPUs!")
    model = nn.DataParallel(model)

# Move the model to GPU
model = model.to("cuda")

# Dummy input for forward pass
```

```
inputs = torch.randn(64, 10).to("cuda")
outputs = model(inputs)
print("Output shape:", outputs.shape)
```

Cloud Environments

For large-scale training, use cloud platforms like AWS, GCP, or Azure.

Example: Google Colab

1. Access Colab at colab.research.google.com.
2. Select Runtime > Change runtime type > GPU.
3. Verify GPU:

python

```
import torch
print("GPU available:", torch.cuda.is_available())
```

2.5 Troubleshooting Installation and Dependency Issues
Common Errors and Fixes

Issue	Cause	Solution
torch module not found	PyTorch not installed correctly	Reinstall using the correct command.
No CUDA runtime found	CUDA not installed or mismatch with PyTorch	Install matching CUDA version.
GPU unavailable in Colab	Runtime not set to GPU	Change runtime type to GPU in Colab.
pip version conflict	Outdated pip or dependency issues	Upgrade pip: pip install --upgrade pip.

Verifying Dependencies

Run the following code to list installed packages and their versions:
bash

```
pip list
```

Updating PyTorch

To upgrade PyTorch, use:
bash

```
pip install --upgrade torch torchvision torchaudio
```

In this chapter, you've learned how to set up PyTorch for both CPU and GPU configurations, install essential libraries like Hugging Face Transformers and PyTorch Lightning, and configure your environment for seamless coding. With these tools in place, you're now ready to dive into building and fine-tuning Large Language Models. Let's get started with the fundamentals of PyTorch in the next chapter!

Code Examples

This section provides detailed code examples to verify PyTorch installation, test Hugging Face Transformers and Datasets, and configure a Colab notebook environment for seamless use. These steps will ensure your environment is fully operational and ready for developing Large Language Models (LLMs).

1. Verifying PyTorch Installation and GPU Availability

Once PyTorch is installed, it's essential to confirm the installation and check whether your system can utilize GPU acceleration.

Step-by-Step Explanation

1. **Verify Installation**: Check the installed version of PyTorch.
2. **Check GPU Availability**: Ensure CUDA is enabled if you have a GPU.
3. **Test with a Simple Tensor Operation**: Create and manipulate tensors to verify functionality.

Code Example

python

```python
import torch

# Verify PyTorch version
print("PyTorch Version:", torch.__version__)

# Check GPU availability
if torch.cuda.is_available():
    print("CUDA is available. GPU can be used.")
    print("GPU Name:", torch.cuda.get_device_name(0))
else:
    print("CUDA is not available. Using CPU.")
```

```
# Simple tensor operation
tensor = torch.rand(3, 3)
print("Random Tensor:\n", tensor)

# Move tensor to GPU if available
if torch.cuda.is_available():
    tensor = tensor.to("cuda")
    print("Tensor on GPU:\n", tensor)
```

Expected Output

- On a GPU-enabled system:

lua

PyTorch Version: 2.x
CUDA is available. GPU can be used.
GPU Name: NVIDIA GeForce RTX 3090
Random Tensor:
 tensor([[0.6741, 0.0206, 0.1129],
        [0.8823, 0.9064, 0.6398],
        [0.2301, 0.9875, 0.3944]])
Tensor on GPU:
 tensor([[0.6741, 0.0206, 0.1129],
        [0.8823, 0.9064, 0.6398],
        [0.2301, 0.9875, 0.3944]], device='cuda:0')

- On a CPU-only system:

lua

PyTorch Version: 2.x
CUDA is not available. Using CPU.
Random Tensor:
 tensor([[0.6741, 0.0206, 0.1129],
        [0.8823, 0.9064, 0.6398],
        [0.2301, 0.9875, 0.3944]])

---

2. Installing and Testing Hugging Face Transformers and Datasets

Hugging Face provides pre-trained models and datasets that simplify working with LLMs. Here's how to install and verify their functionality.

Step-by-Step Explanation

1. **Install Libraries**:

- o Install transformers for models.
- o Install datasets for accessing pre-built datasets.
2. **Load a Pre-Trained Model**: Use Hugging Face pipelines to load a model and test basic functionality.
3. **Access a Dataset**: Load and preview a sample dataset from the Hugging Face datasets library.

Code Example
python

```
# Install Hugging Face libraries
!pip install transformers datasets

# Verify installation by loading a pre-trained model
from transformers import pipeline

# Load a sentiment analysis pipeline
sentiment_analyzer = pipeline("sentiment-analysis")

# Test the pipeline
result = sentiment_analyzer("I love using PyTorch for
AI projects!")
print("Sentiment Analysis Result:", result)

# Access and preview a dataset
from datasets import load_dataset

# Load the IMDB movie reviews dataset
dataset = load_dataset("imdb")

# Preview the dataset
print("Dataset Info:", dataset)
print("Sample Review:", dataset['train'][0])
```

Expected Output
1. Sentiment Analysis:
css

Sentiment Analysis Result: [{'label': 'POSITIVE', 'score': 0.9997}]
2. Dataset Preview:
css

```
Dataset Info: DatasetDict({
    train: Dataset({
        features: ['text', 'label'],
        num_rows: 25000
    })
    test: Dataset({
        features: ['text', 'label'],
        num_rows: 25000
    })
})
```
Sample Review: {'text': "This movie is fantastic! I loved every second of it.", 'label': 1}

---

3. Setting Up a Colab Notebook Environment

Google Colab provides a free, cloud-based platform to run Python code with GPU acceleration. This is particularly useful for working with LLMs without requiring a high-performance local machine.

Step-by-Step Explanation

1. **Access Colab**: Go to Google Colab.
2. **Change Runtime to GPU**:
     - Navigate to Runtime > Change runtime type.
     - Set Hardware Accelerator to GPU.
3. **Install Dependencies**: Use Colab's terminal to install required libraries.
4. **Verify Environment**: Test GPU availability and run sample code.

Code Example

python

```python
# Check GPU availability in Colab
import torch

if torch.cuda.is_available():
    print("Colab is using a GPU!")
    print("GPU Name:", torch.cuda.get_device_name(0))
else:
    print("Colab is not using a GPU. Using CPU.")


# Install Hugging Face libraries
```

```
!pip install transformers datasets

# Test a simple pipeline
from transformers import pipeline

# Load a text-generation pipeline
text_generator = pipeline("text-generation",
model="gpt2")

# Generate text
output = text_generator("PyTorch is a great framework
for", max_length=50)
print("Generated Text:\n", output)
```

Expected Output

1. GPU Availability:

csharp

Colab is using a GPU!
GPU Name: Tesla T4

2. Text Generation:

vbnet

Generated Text:
[{'generated_text': 'PyTorch is a great framework for developing and
deploying machine learning models. Its dynamic computation graph
allows flexibility, making it suitable for both research and production.'}]

With these code examples, you've successfully:
- Verified your PyTorch installation and GPU configuration.
- Installed and tested Hugging Face Transformers and Datasets.
- Configured and tested a Colab notebook environment.

These steps ensure that your development environment is ready for experimenting with PyTorch and LLMs. Let's move on to building foundational skills in the next chapter!

Chapter 3: PyTorch Essentials for LLMs

PyTorch provides a robust and flexible foundation for building, training, and deploying machine learning models, especially Large Language Models (LLMs). This chapter introduces the core components of PyTorch that are essential for understanding and implementing LLMs.

3.1 Tensors: The Building Blocks of PyTorch

Tensors are the primary data structure in PyTorch. They are similar to NumPy arrays but with additional capabilities for GPU acceleration and automatic differentiation.

Key Features of Tensors:
1. **Multidimensional Data**: Tensors can store scalars, vectors, matrices, and higher-dimensional data.
2. **GPU Support**: Tensors can perform operations on GPUs for faster computations.
3. **Flexible Operations**: PyTorch provides a rich set of tensor operations for manipulation and computation.

Code Examples: Working with Tensors
python

```python
import torch

# Create a tensor
tensor = torch.tensor([[1, 2], [3, 4]])
print("Tensor:\n", tensor)

# Create random tensors
rand_tensor = torch.rand(2, 3)
print("Random Tensor:\n", rand_tensor)

# Tensor operations
```

```
sum_tensor = tensor + tensor
print("Summed Tensor:\n", sum_tensor)

# Move tensor to GPU (if available)
if torch.cuda.is_available():
    gpu_tensor = tensor.to("cuda")
    print("Tensor on GPU:\n", gpu_tensor)
```

Expected Output

lua

```
Tensor:
 tensor([[1, 2],
        [3, 4]])
Random Tensor:
 tensor([[0.1234, 0.5678, 0.9101],
        [0.1123, 0.3456, 0.7890]])
Summed Tensor:
 tensor([[2, 4],
        [6, 8]])
Tensor on GPU:
 tensor([[1, 2],
        [3, 4]], device='cuda:0')
```

3.2 Understanding PyTorch's Dynamic Computation Graphs

In PyTorch, the computation graph is dynamically built during runtime. This makes it easy to debug and modify models on the fly.

Key Concepts:
- **Dynamic Graph**: Unlike TensorFlow's static graph, PyTorch creates the graph dynamically, allowing immediate feedback during model execution.
- **Flexibility**: Dynamic graphs make it easier to experiment with different model architectures.

Code Example: Dynamic Graph

python

```
import torch

x = torch.tensor(2.0, requires_grad=True)
y = torch.tensor(3.0, requires_grad=True)

# Define a computation
z = x * y + y
print("Result:", z)

# Compute gradients
z.backward()
print("Gradient of x:", x.grad)
print("Gradient of y:", y.grad)
```

Expected Output

css

```
Result: tensor(9., grad_fn=<AddBackward0>)
Gradient of x: tensor(3.)
Gradient of y: tensor(3.)
```

3.3 Automatic Differentiation and Gradient Tracking with autograd

PyTorch's autograd module automates the computation of gradients, which is essential for optimizing machine learning models.

Key Features:
1. **Automatic Gradient Computation**: Gradients are calculated automatically for tensors with requires_grad=True.
2. **Backpropagation**: The backward() method computes the gradients.

Code Example: Gradient Calculation

python

```
import torch

# Define a tensor
x = torch.tensor(5.0, requires_grad=True)

# Define a function
y = x**2 + 3*x + 7

# Compute gradients
y.backward()
print("Gradient of y with respect to x:", x.grad)
```

Expected Output

css

Gradient of y with respect to x: tensor(13.)

3.4 Modules, Layers, and Building Neural Networks

PyTorch's nn.Module provides a framework for defining and managing neural networks.

Key Components:
- **Modules**: Encapsulate layers and operations.
- **Layers**: Building blocks of a neural network (e.g., Linear, ReLU).
- **Forward Method**: Defines the computation performed at each layer.

Code Example: Simple Neural Network

python

```
import torch
import torch.nn as nn

# Define a neural network
class SimpleNN(nn.Module):
```

```python
    def __init__(self):
        super(SimpleNN, self).__init__()
        self.fc1 = nn.Linear(10, 20)   # Input to
hidden layer
        self.relu = nn.ReLU()          # Activation
function
        self.fc2 = nn.Linear(20, 1)   # Hidden to
output layer

    def forward(self, x):
        x = self.fc1(x)
        x = self.relu(x)
        x = self.fc2(x)
        return x

# Create an instance of the network
model = SimpleNN()
print(model)
```

Expected Output

scss

```
SimpleNN(
  (fc1): Linear(in_features=10, out_features=20, bias=True)
  (relu): ReLU()
  (fc2): Linear(in_features=20, out_features=1, bias=True)
)
```

3.5 Optimizers, Learning Rates, and Loss Functions

Optimizers adjust model weights to minimize the loss function. PyTorch provides built-in optimizers and loss functions.

Key Components:
1. **Loss Functions**: Measure the difference between predictions and actual values.
   o Example: Mean Squared Error (nn.MSELoss).

2. **Optimizers**: Adjust weights to reduce the loss.
   - Example: Stochastic Gradient Descent (torch.optim.SGD).

Code Example: Training Loop

python

```python
import torch.optim as optim

# Define the model, loss, and optimizer
model = SimpleNN()
criterion = nn.MSELoss()
optimizer = optim.SGD(model.parameters(), lr=0.01)

# Dummy data
inputs = torch.randn(32, 10)
targets = torch.randn(32, 1)

# Training loop
for epoch in range(5):
    # Forward pass
    outputs = model(inputs)
    loss = criterion(outputs, targets)

    # Backward pass
    optimizer.zero_grad()
    loss.backward()
    optimizer.step()

    print(f"Epoch [{epoch+1}/5], Loss:
{loss.item():.4f}")
```

Expected Output

less

```
Epoch [1/5], Loss: 0.2678
Epoch [2/5], Loss: 0.2413
...
```

3.6 Working with Datasets and DataLoaders

PyTorch's Dataset and DataLoader classes simplify data management.

Key Features:
1. **Dataset**: Encapsulates data loading and preprocessing.
2. **DataLoader**: Provides batches of data for training.

Code Example: Custom Dataset and DataLoader

python

```python
from torch.utils.data import Dataset, DataLoader

# Define a custom dataset
class CustomDataset(Dataset):
    def __init__(self):
        self.data = torch.randn(100, 10)  # 100
samples, 10 features each
        self.labels = torch.randn(100, 1)  # 100
labels

    def __len__(self):
        return len(self.data)

    def __getitem__(self, idx):
        return self.data[idx], self.labels[idx]

# Create a dataset and dataloader
dataset = CustomDataset()
dataloader = DataLoader(dataset, batch_size=16,
shuffle=True)

# Iterate through the dataloader
for batch_idx, (inputs, labels) in
enumerate(dataloader):
    print(f"Batch {batch_idx+1}: Inputs shape
{inputs.shape}, Labels shape {labels.shape}")
```

Expected Output

css

Batch 1: Inputs shape torch.Size([16, 10]), Labels shape torch.Size([16, 1])
Batch 2: Inputs shape torch.Size([16, 10]), Labels shape torch.Size([16, 1])
...

This chapter introduced you to the core building blocks of PyTorch:
- Tensors for data representation.
- Dynamic computation graphs for flexibility.
- Automatic differentiation for gradient computation.
- Modules, layers, and optimizers for building and training neural networks.

With these fundamentals, you are well-prepared to dive deeper into training and fine-tuning Large Language Models in PyTorch.

Code Examples

This section provides detailed examples demonstrating key PyTorch functionalities essential for developing machine learning models, especially Large Language Models (LLMs). These examples will cover:

1. **Tensor Operations**: Creation, slicing, and reshaping.
2. **Building a Simple Feedforward Neural Network**.
3. **Training a Neural Network with a Custom Loss Function**.

1. Demonstrating Tensor Operations

Tensors are the foundation of PyTorch. Understanding how to create, manipulate, and reshape tensors is critical for working with models.

Step-by-Step Explanation

1. **Creation**: Create tensors with specific shapes and values.
2. **Slicing**: Extract specific portions of a tensor.
3. **Reshaping**: Change the dimensions of a tensor without altering its data.

Code Example
python

```python
import torch

# 1. Tensor Creation
# Create a tensor with specific values
tensor = torch.tensor([[1, 2, 3], [4, 5, 6]])
print("Original Tensor:\n", tensor)

# Create a random tensor
rand_tensor = torch.rand(2, 3)
print("\nRandom Tensor:\n", rand_tensor)

# Create a zero tensor
zero_tensor = torch.zeros(3, 3)
print("\nZero Tensor:\n", zero_tensor)

# 2. Tensor Slicing
# Extract the first row
first_row = tensor[0, :]
print("\nFirst Row:\n", first_row)

# Extract a single element
element = tensor[1, 2]
print("\nSingle Element (Row 2, Column 3):",
element.item())

# 3. Tensor Reshaping
# Reshape the tensor into a single row
reshaped_tensor = tensor.view(1, -1)
print("\nReshaped Tensor (1 row):\n",
reshaped_tensor)

# Transpose the tensor
transposed_tensor = tensor.t()
print("\nTransposed Tensor:\n", transposed_tensor)
```

Expected Output

lua

```
Original Tensor:
tensor([[1, 2, 3],
        [4, 5, 6]])

Random Tensor:
tensor([[0.1234, 0.5678, 0.9101],
        [0.1123, 0.3456, 0.7890]])

Zero Tensor:
tensor([[0., 0., 0.],
        [0., 0., 0.],
        [0., 0., 0.]])

First Row:
tensor([1, 2, 3])

Single Element (Row 2, Column 3): 6

Reshaped Tensor (1 row):
tensor([[1, 2, 3, 4, 5, 6]])

Transposed Tensor:
tensor([[1, 4],
        [2, 5],
        [3, 6]])
```

---

2. Building a Simple Feedforward Neural Network

A feedforward neural network is the simplest form of an artificial neural network. It consists of input, hidden, and output layers where information flows in one direction.

Step-by-Step Explanation

1. **Define the Model**: Use torch.nn.Module to create a custom model.
2. **Layers**: Add fully connected (Linear) layers and activation functions (e.g., ReLU).

3. **Forward Method**: Define how the input flows through the layers.

Code Example

python

```python
import torch.nn as nn

# Define the feedforward neural network
class FeedforwardNN(nn.Module):
    def __init__(self, input_size, hidden_size, output_size):
        super(FeedforwardNN, self).__init__()
        self.fc1 = nn.Linear(input_size, hidden_size)
# Input to hidden layer
        self.relu = nn.ReLU()
# Activation function
        self.fc2 = nn.Linear(hidden_size, output_size)   # Hidden to output layer

    def forward(self, x):
        x = self.fc1(x)
        x = self.relu(x)
        x = self.fc2(x)
        return x

# Create an instance of the network
input_size = 10
hidden_size = 20
output_size = 1
model = FeedforwardNN(input_size, hidden_size, output_size)

# Print the model architecture
print(model)
```

Expected Output

scss

```
FeedforwardNN(
  (fc1): Linear(in_features=10, out_features=20, bias=True)
```

```
(relu): ReLU()
(fc2): Linear(in_features=20, out_features=1,
bias=True)
)
```

---

3. Training a Neural Network with a Custom Loss Function

Training a neural network involves:

1. Defining a loss function to measure errors.
2. Optimizing the network weights to minimize the loss.
3. Backpropagating the gradients.

We will define a custom loss function for this example.

Step-by-Step Explanation

1. **Custom Loss Function**: Implement a custom loss function (e.g., Mean Absolute Error).
2. **Training Loop**: Iterate over multiple epochs to optimize the model.
3. **Optimization**: Use a built-in optimizer like Stochastic Gradient Descent (SGD).

Code Example

python

```python
import torch.optim as optim

# Define a custom loss function
class CustomLoss(nn.Module):
    def __init__(self):
        super(CustomLoss, self).__init__()

    def forward(self, predictions, targets):
        # Mean Absolute Error (L1 Loss)
        loss = torch.mean(torch.abs(predictions -
targets))
        return loss

# Initialize model, custom loss, and optimizer
model = FeedforwardNN(input_size=10, hidden_size=20,
output_size=1)
criterion = CustomLoss()  # Custom loss function
```

```python
optimizer = optim.SGD(model.parameters(), lr=0.01)   #
Optimizer

# Dummy data for training
inputs = torch.randn(32, 10)   # Batch of 32 samples
with 10 features
targets = torch.randn(32, 1)   # Corresponding target
values

# Training loop
for epoch in range(5):
    # Forward pass
    outputs = model(inputs)
    loss = criterion(outputs, targets)

    # Backward pass and optimization
    optimizer.zero_grad()
    loss.backward()
    optimizer.step()

    print(f"Epoch [{epoch+1}/5], Loss:
{loss.item():.4f}")
```

Expected Output

less

Epoch [1/5], Loss: 0.8742
Epoch [2/5], Loss: 0.7123
Epoch [3/5], Loss: 0.6412
Epoch [4/5], Loss: 0.5387
Epoch [5/5], Loss: 0.4891

- **Tensor Operations**: You learned how to create, slice, and reshape tensors, the core building blocks of PyTorch.
- **Feedforward Neural Network**: You built a simple network with fully connected layers and activation functions.
- **Custom Loss Function**: You implemented a custom loss function and trained the network using a straightforward training loop.

These examples lay the groundwork for more complex neural network models, including those used in Large Language Models (LLMs).

Chapter 4: Foundations of Transformer Architectures

Transformers are the backbone of modern NLP, powering models like GPT, BERT, and T5. They marked a paradigm shift in how language models process and understand text, outperforming previous approaches like RNNs and LSTMs. This chapter delves into their evolution, key components, and implementations, culminating in building a mini Transformer from scratch in PyTorch.

4.1 The Evolution from RNNs to Transformers

What Are RNNs?

Recurrent Neural Networks (RNNs) process input sequences token by token while maintaining a hidden state that captures context. They were the standard for NLP tasks such as machine translation and text generation.

Limitations of RNNs:

1. **Sequential Processing**:
   o Tokens must be processed one after another, making training and inference slow.
2. **Vanishing Gradients**:
   o Gradients diminish over long sequences, making it hard to capture long-range dependencies.
3. **Limited Parallelism**:
   o Since each step depends on the previous one, training cannot be parallelized efficiently.

Why Transformers?

Transformers, introduced in the seminal paper *"Attention is All You Need"* (Vaswani et al., 2017), address these limitations by:

- Leveraging **self-attention** to process all tokens simultaneously.
- Enabling efficient parallelization using attention mechanisms.
- Capturing long-range dependencies effectively without relying on sequential updates.

4.2 Anatomy of a Transformer

A Transformer model consists of **encoder** and **decoder** layers, with self-attention and feedforward networks as core components.

Key Components:

1. Self-Attention Mechanism

Self-attention computes relationships between all tokens in a sequence to determine which tokens are most relevant to each other.

1. **Query, Key, and Value (Q, K, V):**
   - Each input token is transformed into three vectors:
     - **Query (Q):** What the token is looking for.
     - **Key (K):** What the token has.
     - **Value (V):** The information the token carries.
2. **Attention Scores:**
   - Compute the relevance of tokens using a dot product between the Query and Key vectors.

   Scale the scores and apply a softmax function to normalize them:

$$Attention(Q,K,V) = softmax\left(\frac{QK^T}{\sqrt{d_k}}\right)V$$

3. **Weighted Sum:**
   - Combine the values (V) based on the attention scores to produce the final output.

Code Example: Self-Attention Mechanism

python

```
import torch
import torch.nn.functional as F

# Define Query, Key, and Value
Q = torch.tensor([[1.0, 0.0], [0.0, 1.0]])   # 2x2
matrix
K = torch.tensor([[1.0, 0.5], [0.5, 1.0]])   # 2x2
matrix
V = torch.tensor([[1.0, 2.0], [3.0, 4.0]])   # 2x2
matrix
```

```
# Compute Attention Scores
scores = torch.matmul(Q, K.T) /
torch.sqrt(torch.tensor(K.shape[-1],
dtype=torch.float32))
attention_weights = F.softmax(scores, dim=-1)

# Compute Weighted Sum
output = torch.matmul(attention_weights, V)
print("Attention Output:\n", output)
Expected Output:
lua
```

```
Attention Output:
 tensor([[1.7500, 3.0000],
         [2.5000, 3.5000]])
```

---

2. Multi-Head Attention

Instead of a single attention mechanism, **multi-head attention** uses multiple attention heads to learn different types of relationships between tokens.

1. **Parallel Attention**:
    o   Each head performs self-attention independently.
2. **Concatenation and Projection**:
    o   Combine the outputs of all heads and project them back into the model's dimension.

Advantages:

*   Captures diverse relationships between tokens (e.g., syntactic and semantic).

3. Position Encodings and Embeddings

Transformers lack recurrence or convolution, so they need **positional encodings** to account for the order of tokens.

1. **Learned or Fixed Encodings**:
    o   Add positional information to token embeddings.
2. **Sine and Cosine Encoding**:
    o   Encode positions using sine and cosine functions of different frequencies:

$$PE(pos,2i) = sin\left(\frac{pos}{10000^{2i/d}}\right)$$

$$PE(pos, 2i + 1) = cos\left(\frac{pos}{10000^{2i/d}}\right)$$

Code Example: Positional Encoding

python

```
import torch
import math

def positional_encoding(seq_len, d_model):
    PE = torch.zeros(seq_len, d_model)
    for pos in range(seq_len):
        for i in range(0, d_model, 2):
            PE[pos, i] = math.sin(pos / (10000 ** ((2
* i) / d_model)))
            PE[pos, i + 1] = math.cos(pos / (10000 **
((2 * i) / d_model)))
    return PE

# Generate positional encodings
pe = positional_encoding(seq_len=10, d_model=16)
print("Positional Encoding:\n", pe)
```

4.3 Key Transformer Architectures

1. **GPT (Generative Pre-trained Transformer)**:
   - Focus: Text generation.
   - Architecture: Decoder-only.
   - Example: ChatGPT, GPT-4.
2. **BERT (Bidirectional Encoder Representations from Transformers)**:
   - Focus: Understanding context (text classification, Q&A).
   - Architecture: Encoder-only.
   - Example: Hugging Face's bert-base-uncased.
3. **T5 (Text-to-Text Transfer Transformer)**:
   - Focus: Text-to-text tasks (summarization, translation).
   - Architecture: Encoder-decoder.
   - Example: Hugging Face's t5-small.

4.4 Implementing a Mini Transformer Model from Scratch in PyTorch

Step-by-Step Implementation
1. **Define the Model Architecture**:
   o Include an embedding layer, positional encoding, multi-head attention, and feedforward layers.
2. **Code Example**:

python

```python
import torch
import torch.nn as nn

class MiniTransformer(nn.Module):
    def __init__(self, seq_len, d_model, num_heads):
        super(MiniTransformer, self).__init__()
        self.embedding = nn.Embedding(seq_len,
d_model)
        self.pos_encoding =
positional_encoding(seq_len, d_model)
        self.attention =
nn.MultiheadAttention(embed_dim=d_model,
num_heads=num_heads)
        self.fc = nn.Sequential(
            nn.Linear(d_model, 64),
            nn.ReLU(),
            nn.Linear(64, d_model)
        )

    def forward(self, x):
        # Add positional encoding to embeddings
        x = self.embedding(x) + self.pos_encoding
        x = x.transpose(0, 1)   # Required for
MultiheadAttention
        x, _ = self.attention(x, x, x)   # Self-
attention
        x = x.transpose(0, 1)
```

```python
        x = self.fc(x)   # Feedforward layer
        return x

# Instantiate and test the model
seq_len, d_model, num_heads = 10, 16, 2
model = MiniTransformer(seq_len, d_model, num_heads)

# Input sequence
input_seq = torch.randint(0, seq_len, (2, seq_len))
# Batch of 2 sequences
output = model(input_seq)
print("Transformer Output Shape:", output.shape)
Expected Output:
css

Transformer Output Shape: torch.Size([2, 10, 16])
```

In this chapter, we explored:
1. The transition from RNNs to Transformers.
2. Key components of Transformers: self-attention, multi-head attention, and positional encodings.
3. A comparison of popular Transformer architectures.
4. A mini Transformer implementation in PyTorch.

These foundations will prepare you to fine-tune and deploy more complex Transformer-based models.

Code Examples

This section provides step-by-step implementations of the **self-attention mechanism** and a **basic Transformer encoder in PyTorch**. These are the foundational components of the Transformer architecture and critical for understanding and building Transformer-based models.

1. Step-by-Step Implementation of the Self-Attention Mechanism
Overview

Self-attention enables a model to assign dynamic weights to tokens in a sequence based on their relevance to one another. It forms the foundation of Transformers by allowing each token to "attend" to all other tokens.

Steps to Implement Self-Attention:
1. **Compute Query (Q), Key (K), and Value (V):**
   - Transform the input sequence into three matrices: Q, K, and V.
   - These represent what the token is looking for (Q), the information other tokens have (K), and the token's own content (V).
2. **Calculate Attention Scores:**
   - Perform a dot product between Q and K to calculate similarity.
   - Scale the scores by dividing by the square root of the embedding size (dk\sqrt{d_k}dk) to stabilize gradients.
3. **Apply Softmax:**
   - Normalize the scores into probabilities.
4. **Compute Weighted Sum:**
   - Multiply the Value matrix (V) by the attention scores to produce the output.

Code Example: Self-Attention Mechanism
python

```
import torch
import torch.nn.functional as F

# Define input sequence
batch_size = 2
seq_len = 4
embedding_dim = 8

# Random input tensor (batch of sequences)
inputs = torch.randn(batch_size, seq_len,
embedding_dim)

# Define weight matrices for Query, Key, and Value
W_q = torch.randn(embedding_dim, embedding_dim)
W_k = torch.randn(embedding_dim, embedding_dim)
W_v = torch.randn(embedding_dim, embedding_dim)

# Compute Query, Key, and Value
```

```
Q = torch.matmul(inputs, W_q)   # (batch_size,
seq_len, embedding_dim)
K = torch.matmul(inputs, W_k)   # (batch_size,
seq_len, embedding_dim)
V = torch.matmul(inputs, W_v)   # (batch_size,
seq_len, embedding_dim)

# Step 2: Compute scaled dot-product attention scores
scores = torch.matmul(Q, K.transpose(-2, -1)) /
torch.sqrt(torch.tensor(embedding_dim,
dtype=torch.float32))
print("Attention Scores:\n", scores)

# Step 3: Apply softmax to normalize scores
attention_weights = F.softmax(scores, dim=-1)
print("\nAttention Weights:\n", attention_weights)

# Step 4: Compute weighted sum of values
output = torch.matmul(attention_weights, V)
print("\nSelf-Attention Output:\n", output)
```

Expected Output
1. **Attention Scores**:
    o A tensor of raw similarity scores between tokens.
2. **Attention Weights**:
    o Normalized probabilities indicating the importance of each
       token relative to others.
3. **Self-Attention Output**:
    o Weighted sum of the values for each token.

---

2. Building a Basic Transformer Encoder in PyTorch
Overview
The Transformer encoder processes a sequence of tokens and outputs
contextualized embeddings using layers of:
1. **Multi-Head Self-Attention**: Multiple attention heads capture
   different relationships between tokens.
2. **Feedforward Neural Network**: Processes the output of the
   attention mechanism.

3. **Add & Norm Layers**: Ensure stability by adding residual connections and normalizing outputs.

Code Example: Transformer Encoder
python

```python
import torch
import torch.nn as nn

class TransformerEncoderLayer(nn.Module):
    def __init__(self, embedding_dim, num_heads,
ff_dim, dropout=0.1):
        super(TransformerEncoderLayer,
self).__init__()
        # Multi-Head Self-Attention
        self.self_attention =
nn.MultiheadAttention(embed_dim=embedding_dim,
num_heads=num_heads)
        # Feedforward Neural Network
        self.feedforward = nn.Sequential(
            nn.Linear(embedding_dim, ff_dim),
            nn.ReLU(),
            nn.Linear(ff_dim, embedding_dim)
        )
        # Add & Norm Layers
        self.norm1 = nn.LayerNorm(embedding_dim)
        self.norm2 = nn.LayerNorm(embedding_dim)
        self.dropout = nn.Dropout(dropout)

    def forward(self, x):
        # Self-Attention
        attention_output, _ = self.self_attention(x,
x, x)
        x = self.norm1(x +
self.dropout(attention_output))   # Add & Norm

        # Feedforward
        ff_output = self.feedforward(x)
```

```python
        x = self.norm2(x + self.dropout(ff_output))
# Add & Norm

        return x

# Instantiate and test the Transformer Encoder
seq_len = 10
embedding_dim = 16
num_heads = 2
ff_dim = 32

# Input tensor (sequence of embedded tokens)
inputs = torch.randn(seq_len, batch_size,
embedding_dim)  # Note: seq_len comes first for
attention layers

# Define Transformer Encoder Layer
encoder_layer =
TransformerEncoderLayer(embedding_dim, num_heads,
ff_dim)

# Forward pass
outputs = encoder_layer(inputs)
print("Transformer Encoder Output Shape:",
outputs.shape)
Expected Output
css


Transformer Encoder Output Shape: torch.Size([10, 2,
16])
```

Detailed Explanation of Code
1. Multi-Head Self-Attention Layer
- The nn.MultiheadAttention module handles multi-head self-attention in PyTorch.
- Input shape: (seq_len, batch_size, embedding_dim).
- Output:
  - Contextualized embeddings for each token.
2. Feedforward Neural Network

- A two-layer MLP processes the attention output:
  - Expands embeddings to a higher dimension (ff_dim).
  - Projects back to the original embedding size.

3. Add & Norm
- **Residual Connections**:
  - Add the input back to the output for stability.
- **Layer Normalization**:
  - Normalizes the output for efficient gradient flow.

In this section, we:
1. Implemented the **self-attention mechanism** step by step.
2. Built a **basic Transformer encoder layer** with self-attention, feedforward layers, and normalization.

These components form the foundation of Transformer models, enabling them to process and contextualize sequential data efficiently. This knowledge prepares you for creating more complex architectures like GPT, BERT, and T5

Chapter 5: Preparing Data for LLMs

Preparing data is a crucial step in training and fine-tuning Large Language Models (LLMs). This chapter provides a comprehensive guide to tokenization, preprocessing text data, leveraging Hugging Face datasets, building custom tokenizers, and applying data augmentation techniques for improved model performance.

5.1 Tokenization Basics

Tokenization is the process of splitting text into smaller units (tokens) that can be processed by a machine learning model. Tokenization ensures the model can effectively work with language input, even for rare or unknown words.

Types of Tokenization
1. **Byte-Pair Encoding (BPE)**:
   o A subword tokenization technique that iteratively merges the most frequent byte pairs.
   o Balances vocabulary size and representation granularity.
   o Example: "uncommon" → ["un", "common"].
2. **WordPiece**:
   o Similar to BPE but uses probabilistic criteria for merging.
   o Used in models like BERT.
   o Example: "running" → ["run", "##ning"] (## denotes subwords).
3. **SentencePiece**:
   o Tokenizes text into subwords or characters without requiring whitespace splitting.
   o Used in models like T5.
   o Example: "Tokenizer" → ["_Token", "izer"] (_ represents a space).

Code Example: Tokenizing Text with Hugging Face Tokenizers
python

```
from transformers import AutoTokenizer
```

```
# Load a pre-trained tokenizer (e.g., BERT)
tokenizer = AutoTokenizer.from_pretrained("bert-base-
uncased")

# Tokenize a sentence
sentence = "Transformers are amazing for NLP tasks!"
tokens = tokenizer.tokenize(sentence)
print("Tokens:", tokens)

# Convert tokens to IDs
token_ids = tokenizer.convert_tokens_to_ids(tokens)
print("Token IDs:", token_ids)

# Decode token IDs back to text
decoded_sentence = tokenizer.decode(token_ids)
print("Decoded Sentence:", decoded_sentence)
```

Expected Output
sql

Tokens: ['transformers', 'are', 'amazing', 'for', 'nl', '##p', 'tasks', '!']
Token IDs: [19081, 2024, 6429, 2005, 17953, 2361, 8184, 999]
Decoded Sentence: transformers are amazing for nlp tasks!

5.2 Preprocessing Text Data for Training and Fine-Tuning

Key Preprocessing Steps
1. **Lowercasing and Removing Special Characters**:
   - Normalize text to reduce variability.
   - Example: Convert "Hello, WORLD!" to "hello world".
2. **Tokenization**:
   - Split text into tokens using the appropriate tokenizer.
3. **Padding and Truncation**:
   - Pad sequences to a fixed length for batch processing.
   - Truncate long sequences to avoid memory overflow.
4. **Encoding**:

        ○   Convert tokens into numerical IDs for model processing.

Code Example: Text Preprocessing

python

```python
from transformers import AutoTokenizer

# Load tokenizer
tokenizer = AutoTokenizer.from_pretrained("bert-base-uncased")

# Sample text data
texts = ["Transformers are amazing!", "I love PyTorch."]

# Tokenize, pad, and truncate
encoded_inputs = tokenizer(
    texts,
    max_length=10,
    padding="max_length",
    truncation=True,
    return_tensors="pt"
)

print("Input IDs:\n", encoded_inputs["input_ids"])
print("Attention Masks:\n",
encoded_inputs["attention_mask"])
```

Expected Output

lua

```lua
Input IDs:
 tensor([[19081, 2024, 6429,    0,    0,    0,    0,    0,    0,    0],
     [ 1045, 2293, 20167, 1012,    0,    0,    0,    0,    0,    0]])
Attention Masks:
 tensor([[1, 1, 1, 0, 0, 0, 0, 0, 0, 0],
     [1, 1, 1, 1, 0, 0, 0, 0, 0, 0]])
```

5.3 Using Hugging Face Datasets for Large-Scale Text Data

The Hugging Face datasets library provides access to ready-to-use NLP datasets.

Steps to Use Hugging Face Datasets
1. **Load Dataset**:
   o Load datasets like IMDB or Wikipedia directly.
2. **Inspect and Process**:
   o Examine dataset structure and preprocess text data.
3. **Dataset Operations**:
   o Filter, map, and batch data for training.

Code Example: Working with Hugging Face Datasets
python

```python
from datasets import load_dataset

# Load IMDB dataset
dataset = load_dataset("imdb")

# Inspect the dataset
print("Dataset Structure:\n", dataset)

# Access train and test data
train_data = dataset["train"]
print("Sample Training Data:", train_data[0])

# Tokenize dataset
from transformers import AutoTokenizer

tokenizer = AutoTokenizer.from_pretrained("bert-base-uncased")

def preprocess_data(example):
    return tokenizer(
        example["text"],
        max_length=128,
```

```
        padding="max_length",
        truncation=True
    )


# Apply tokenization to the dataset
tokenized_dataset = dataset.map(preprocess_data,
batched=True)
print("Tokenized Sample:",
tokenized_dataset["train"][0])
```

5.4 Building Custom Tokenizers in PyTorch

For domain-specific tasks, building a custom tokenizer allows you to adapt the tokenization process to your data.

Steps to Build a Custom Tokenizer:
1. Create a vocabulary of unique tokens from the dataset.
2. Implement a tokenization function.
3. Map tokens to IDs and handle padding/truncation.

Code Example: Custom Tokenizer
python

```python
import re


# Define custom tokenizer
class CustomTokenizer:
    def __init__(self, vocab):
        self.vocab = vocab
        self.token_to_id = {token: idx for idx, token
in enumerate(vocab)}

    def tokenize(self, text):
        tokens = re.findall(r"\w+|[^\w\s]",
text.lower())
        return tokens

    def encode(self, tokens):
        return [self.token_to_id.get(token,
self.token_to_id["<UNK>"]) for token in tokens]
```

```
# Vocabulary
vocab = ["<PAD>", "<UNK>", "transformers", "are",
"amazing", "for", "nlp", "tasks", "!"]
tokenizer = CustomTokenizer(vocab)

# Tokenize and encode a sample text
text = "Transformers are amazing for NLP tasks!"
tokens = tokenizer.tokenize(text)
encoded_tokens = tokenizer.encode(tokens)

print("Tokens:", tokens)
print("Encoded Tokens:", encoded_tokens)
Expected Output
arduino


Tokens: ['transformers', 'are', 'amazing', 'for',
'nlp', 'tasks', '!']
Encoded Tokens: [2, 3, 4, 5, 6, 7, 8]
```

5.5 Data Augmentation for Robust Model Performance

Data augmentation improves model generalization by artificially increasing dataset diversity.

Techniques for NLP:

1. **Synonym Replacement**:
   - Replace words with their synonyms.
2. **Random Insertion/Deletion**:
   - Insert or delete random words in the text.
3. **Back-Translation**:
   - Translate text to another language and back to introduce variation.

Code Example: Synonym Replacement

python

```
import random
```

```python
from nltk.corpus import wordnet

# Replace a word with a synonym
def synonym_replacement(text):
    words = text.split()
    new_words = []
    for word in words:
        synonyms = wordnet.synsets(word)
        if synonyms:
            synonym =
random.choice(synonyms).lemmas()[0].name()
            new_words.append(synonym)
        else:
            new_words.append(word)
    return " ".join(new_words)

# Apply to a sample sentence
sentence = "Transformers are amazing for NLP tasks."
augmented_sentence = synonym_replacement(sentence)
print("Original Sentence:", sentence)
print("Augmented Sentence:", augmented_sentence)
```

Expected Output
rust

Original Sentence: Transformers are amazing for NLP tasks.
Augmented Sentence: Transformers are astonishing for NLP jobs.

This chapter equips you with essential tools and techniques for preparing data for LLMs:
1. Tokenization basics (BPE, WordPiece, SentencePiece).
2. Preprocessing techniques for effective training.
3. Leveraging Hugging Face datasets for scalable data pipelines.
4. Building custom tokenizers for domain-specific tasks.
5. Using data augmentation to enhance model robustness.

These techniques ensure your data pipeline is robust, efficient, and ready for training large-scale LLMs.

Code Examples

This section provides detailed and comprehensive examples for key tasks in NLP data preprocessing:

1. **Tokenizing a Text Dataset using Hugging Face Tokenizers**: We'll use Hugging Face's transformers library to tokenize a text dataset.
2. **Writing a Custom PyTorch Dataset Class for Text Preprocessing**: We'll build a custom Dataset class for efficient text preprocessing and loading.
3. **Data Augmentation Techniques for NLP Tasks**: We'll explore common data augmentation methods for improving model generalization.

---

1. Tokenizing a Text Dataset using Hugging Face Tokenizers

Hugging Face provides a powerful and easy-to-use transformers library, which includes pre-built tokenizers for a wide variety of models. Tokenization is essential to convert raw text into a format that models can process.

Step-by-Step Explanation

1. **Load a Pre-trained Tokenizer**: We use a tokenizer specific to the model, such as BERT or GPT.
2. **Tokenize the Text Dataset**: Apply the tokenizer to the entire dataset.
3. **Handle Padding and Truncation**: Pad or truncate sequences to a fixed length for consistency.

Code Example

python

```python
from transformers import AutoTokenizer
from datasets import load_dataset

# Load the IMDB dataset from Hugging Face Datasets
dataset = load_dataset("imdb")

# Load pre-trained tokenizer (e.g., BERT tokenizer)
tokenizer = AutoTokenizer.from_pretrained("bert-base-uncased")
```

```python
# Define a function to preprocess the data
def tokenize_function(examples):
    return tokenizer(
        examples["text"],
        padding="max_length",  # Pad to the maximum
length
        truncation=True,        # Truncate sequences
that are too long
        max_length=128          # Set the maximum
sequence length
    )

# Tokenize the train and test datasets
tokenized_dataset = dataset.map(tokenize_function,
batched=True)

# Display a sample of the tokenized data
print("Sample tokenized data:",
tokenized_dataset["train"][0])
```

Expected Output
python

```
Sample tokenized data: {
    'input_ids': [101, 2465, 1045, 2023, 2204, 2339,
1029, 102, 0, 0, 0, 0, 0, 0, 0, 0, 0, 0, 0, 0],
    'attention_mask': [1, 1, 1, 1, 1, 1, 1, 1, 0, 0,
0, 0, 0, 0, 0, 0, 0, 0, 0, 0],
    'label': 1
}
```

Explanation:
- **input_ids**: The tokenized representation of the input text.
- **attention_mask**: Indicates which tokens are padding (0) and which are real tokens (1).
- **label**: The sentiment label for the text.

2. Writing a Custom PyTorch Dataset Class for Text Preprocessing

When working with custom datasets, it's often necessary to write a custom Dataset class in PyTorch. This class defines how to preprocess and load the data for training.

Step-by-Step Explanation
1. **Create a Custom Dataset Class**: Inherit from torch.utils.data.Dataset.
2. **Override __len__ and __getitem__:**
   - __len__: Returns the size of the dataset.
   - __getitem__: Defines how to retrieve each sample.
3. **Preprocessing**: Apply tokenization and padding within the __getitem__ method.

Code Example

python

```python
import torch
from torch.utils.data import Dataset
from transformers import AutoTokenizer

class CustomTextDataset(Dataset):
    def __init__(self, texts, labels, tokenizer_name,
max_length=128):
        self.texts = texts
        self.labels = labels
        self.tokenizer =
AutoTokenizer.from_pretrained(tokenizer_name)
        self.max_length = max_length

    def __len__(self):
        return len(self.texts)

    def __getitem__(self, idx):
        text = self.texts[idx]
        label = self.labels[idx]

        # Tokenize the text
        encoding = self.tokenizer(
            text,
```

```python
            truncation=True,
            padding="max_length",
            max_length=self.max_length,
            return_tensors="pt"
        )

        # Return input_ids, attention_mask, and label
        return {
            "input_ids":
encoding["input_ids"].squeeze(0),
            "attention_mask":
encoding["attention_mask"].squeeze(0),
            "label": torch.tensor(label,
dtype=torch.long)
        }

# Example usage with sample data
texts = ["Transformers are powerful!", "I love
working with PyTorch."]
labels = [1, 0]  # Example labels (e.g., 1 for
positive, 0 for negative)

dataset = CustomTextDataset(texts, labels, "bert-
base-uncased")

# Accessing a sample
sample = dataset[0]
print("Sample data:", sample)
```

Expected Output

python

```
Sample data: {
   'input_ids': tensor([101, 2465, 2023, 2204, 2339, 1029, 102, 0, 0, 0, 0,
0, 0, 0, 0, 0, 0, 0, 0, 0]),
   'attention_mask': tensor([1, 1, 1, 1, 1, 1, 1, 0, 0, 0, 0, 0, 0, 0, 0, 0, 0, 0, 0,
0, 0]),
   'label': tensor(1)
}
```

Explanation:
- **input_ids**: The tokenized representation of the text.
- **attention_mask**: Shows the padding tokens.
- **label**: The sentiment label for the text (1 for positive sentiment, 0 for negative).

3. Data Augmentation Techniques for NLP Tasks

Data augmentation in NLP can help improve model generalization by introducing variety into the training data. Common techniques include synonym replacement, random insertion, and back-translation.

Step-by-Step Explanation

1. **Synonym Replacement**:
   - Randomly replace words in a sentence with their synonyms.
2. **Random Insertion**:
   - Randomly insert new words into the sentence.
3. **Back-Translation**:
   - Translate the text to another language and back, generating varied phrasing.

Code Example: Synonym Replacement

python

```
import random
from nltk.corpus import wordnet

# Synonym replacement function
def synonym_replacement(text):
    words = text.split()
    new_words = []
    for word in words:
        synonyms = wordnet.synsets(word)
        if synonyms:
            synonym =
random.choice(synonyms).lemmas()[0].name()
            new_words.append(synonym)
        else:
            new_words.append(word)
    return " ".join(new_words)
```

```python
# Sample sentence for augmentation
sentence = "Transformers are amazing for NLP tasks."
augmented_sentence = synonym_replacement(sentence)
print("Original Sentence:", sentence)
print("Augmented Sentence:", augmented_sentence)
```
Expected Output
python

Original Sentence: Transformers are amazing for NLP tasks.
Augmented Sentence: Transformers are stunning for NLP jobs.

Code Example: Random Insertion
python

```python
def random_insertion(text):
    words = text.split()
    new_word = "deep"
    random_index = random.randint(0, len(words)-1)
    words.insert(random_index, new_word)
    return " ".join(words)
```

```python
# Sample sentence for random insertion
sentence = "Transformers are amazing for NLP tasks."
augmented_sentence = random_insertion(sentence)
print("Original Sentence:", sentence)
print("Augmented Sentence:", augmented_sentence)
```
Expected Output
python

Original Sentence: Transformers are amazing for NLP tasks.
Augmented Sentence: Transformers are deep amazing for NLP tasks.

Code Example: Back-Translation (using Google Translate API)
python

```python
from googletrans import Translator

# Back-translation function
```

```python
def back_translation(text, src_lang='en',
tgt_lang='fr'):
    translator = Translator()
    translated = translator.translate(text,
src=src_lang, dest=tgt_lang)
    back_translated =
translator.translate(translated.text, src=tgt_lang,
dest=src_lang)
    return back_translated.text

# Example sentence for back-translation
sentence = "Transformers are amazing for NLP tasks."
back_translated_sentence = back_translation(sentence)
print("Original Sentence:", sentence)
print("Back-translated Sentence:",
back_translated_sentence)
```

Expected Output

python

Original Sentence: Transformers are amazing for NLP tasks.
Back-translated Sentence: Transformers sont étonnants pour les tâches NLP.

Chapter 6: Training Large Language Models from Scratch

Training Large Language Models (LLMs) from scratch is an intricate and resource-intensive task that requires a solid understanding of deep learning architectures and best practices. This chapter will guide you through the process of designing Transformer-based architectures in PyTorch, implementing training loops, setting up learning rate schedulers, utilizing distributed training, and avoiding common pitfalls during the training process.

6.1 Designing Transformer-Based Architectures in PyTorch

The Transformer architecture consists of both **encoders** and **decoders**, each containing layers of **self-attention** and **feed-forward networks**. In this section, we will focus on designing a simple Transformer architecture for language tasks. We'll cover the key components: multi-head attention, position-wise feed-forward networks, and layer normalization.

Key Components of Transformer Models:
1. **Multi-Head Attention**: This mechanism allows the model to focus on different parts of the input sequence simultaneously. It learns different types of attention (e.g., syntactic, semantic) for better performance.
2. **Feed-Forward Network**: After attention, the data flows through a position-wise feed-forward network to make predictions.
3. **Add & Norm**: Residual connections are added before layer normalization to stabilize training and allow deeper architectures.

Steps to Build a Basic Transformer Model:
1. Define the **Embedding Layer**: Convert input tokens into embeddings.
2. Define the **Encoder Layer**: Each layer contains multi-head attention followed by a feed-forward network.

3. Implement the **Full Model**: Stack multiple encoder layers to form the Transformer model.

Code Example: Basic Transformer Encoder in PyTorch

python

```python
import torch
import torch.nn as nn

class TransformerEncoderLayer(nn.Module):
    def __init__(self, embedding_dim, num_heads,
ff_dim, dropout=0.1):
        super(TransformerEncoderLayer,
self).__init__()
        # Multi-Head Attention Layer
        self.attention =
nn.MultiheadAttention(embed_dim=embedding_dim,
num_heads=num_heads)

        # Feedforward Neural Network
        self.feedforward = nn.Sequential(
            nn.Linear(embedding_dim, ff_dim),
            nn.ReLU(),
            nn.Linear(ff_dim, embedding_dim)
        )

        # Layer Normalization and Dropout
        self.norm1 = nn.LayerNorm(embedding_dim)
        self.norm2 = nn.LayerNorm(embedding_dim)
        self.dropout = nn.Dropout(dropout)

    def forward(self, x):
        # Attention and Add & Norm
        attn_output, _ = self.attention(x, x, x)
        x = self.norm1(x + self.dropout(attn_output))

        # Feedforward and Add & Norm
        ff_output = self.feedforward(x)
        x = self.norm2(x + self.dropout(ff_output))
```

```
        return x

# Parameters
embedding_dim = 64
num_heads = 4
ff_dim = 128

# Example input (batch_size=2, seq_len=10,
embedding_dim=64)
inputs = torch.randn(10, 2, embedding_dim)

# Instantiate the transformer encoder layer
encoder_layer =
TransformerEncoderLayer(embedding_dim, num_heads,
ff_dim)

# Apply to inputs
output = encoder_layer(inputs)
print("Transformer Encoder Output Shape:",
output.shape)
```

Explanation:
- **MultiheadAttention**: Applies self-attention over the input sequence.
- **Feedforward Network**: A simple MLP with ReLU activation after the attention layer.
- **Residual Connections**: Added before layer normalization for better gradient flow.

Expected Output:
css

Transformer Encoder Output Shape: torch.Size([10, 2, 64])

6.2 Writing Training Loops and Implementing Learning Rate Schedulers

The training loop is where the model is optimized. This includes:
1. **Forward Pass**: Passing inputs through the model.

2. **Loss Computation**: Calculating how far the predictions are from the ground truth.
3. **Backward Pass**: Computing gradients and updating model weights using an optimizer.

Learning Rate Schedulers:
Learning rate schedulers adjust the learning rate during training to help the model converge more efficiently. Common strategies include:
- **Step LR Scheduler**: Reduces the learning rate after a certain number of epochs.
- **Cosine Annealing**: Gradually decays the learning rate from an initial value to a minimum.

Code Example: Training Loop with Learning Rate Scheduler
python

```python
import torch.optim as optim
from torch.optim.lr_scheduler import StepLR

# Model, Loss Function, and Optimizer
model = TransformerEncoderLayer(embedding_dim=64,
num_heads=4, ff_dim=128)
criterion = nn.CrossEntropyLoss()  # Example loss
function for classification tasks
optimizer = optim.Adam(model.parameters(), lr=0.001)

# Learning Rate Scheduler (StepLR)
scheduler = StepLR(optimizer, step_size=10,
gamma=0.5)  # Reduces LR by a factor of 0.5 every 10
epochs

# Dummy input and target for demonstration
inputs = torch.randn(10, 2, 64)  # Example batch
targets = torch.randint(0, 2, (10, 2))  # Example
targets (classification)

# Training loop
epochs = 20
for epoch in range(epochs):
```

```
model.train()  # Set model to training mode

# Forward pass
outputs = model(inputs)
loss = criterion(outputs.view(-1, 64),
targets.view(-1))  # Flatten the output for loss
computation

# Backward pass
optimizer.zero_grad()
loss.backward()
optimizer.step()

# Step the scheduler
scheduler.step()

# Print the loss and current learning rate
print(f"Epoch [{epoch+1}/{epochs}], Loss:
{loss.item():.4f}, LR:
{scheduler.get_last_lr()[0]:.5f}")
```

Explanation:
- **StepLR**: Reduces the learning rate every 10 epochs by a factor of 0.5.
- **Training Loop**: Performs forward and backward passes, updates the model's weights, and adjusts the learning rate.

6.3 Distributed Training with PyTorch

Distributed training allows you to scale up the training process across multiple GPUs or even multiple nodes in a cluster. There are two primary types of parallelism:
1. **Data Parallelism**: Each GPU receives a subset of the data and computes gradients. Gradients are averaged and shared across GPUs.
2. **Model Parallelism**: Different parts of the model are placed on different GPUs. This is useful for very large models that don't fit in memory on a single GPU.

Code Example: Using DataParallel for Multi-GPU Training
python

```python
# Check if multiple GPUs are available
device = torch.device("cuda" if
torch.cuda.is_available() else "cpu")
model = model.to(device)

# Wrap the model with DataParallel for multi-GPU
support
if torch.cuda.device_count() > 1:
    print(f"Using {torch.cuda.device_count()} GPUs!")
    model = nn.DataParallel(model)

# Continue with the training loop...
```

Explanation:
- **nn.DataParallel**: Distributes the input across multiple GPUs and automatically handles synchronization of gradients.

6.4 Avoiding Training Pitfalls

Training large models can be prone to several issues that can impede the learning process or degrade model performance. Here are some common pitfalls and how to mitigate them:

1. **Gradient Clipping**:
   - Helps prevent exploding gradients by clipping gradients that exceed a certain threshold.
   - Useful when training deep networks or models with long sequences.
2. **Overfitting**:
   - Overfitting occurs when the model memorizes the training data but performs poorly on new, unseen data.
   - Use **early stopping**, **dropout**, and **regularization** to mitigate overfitting.
3. **Vanishing Gradients**:
   - Can occur with deep networks, where gradients become too small to update weights.

- o Using **ReLU activations** or **batch normalization** can help alleviate this.

Code Example: Gradient Clipping and Dropout

python

```python
# Gradient Clipping
torch.nn.utils.clip_grad_norm_(model.parameters(),
max_norm=1.0)  # Clip gradients if they exceed 1.0

# Dropout in the model
class TransformerWithDropout(nn.Module):
    def __init__(self, embedding_dim, num_heads,
ff_dim, dropout=0.1):
        super(TransformerWithDropout,
self).__init__()
        self.attention =
nn.MultiheadAttention(embedding_dim, num_heads)
        self.feedforward = nn.Sequential(
            nn.Linear(embedding_dim, ff_dim),
            nn.ReLU(),
            nn.Linear(ff_dim, embedding_dim)
        )
        self.dropout = nn.Dropout(dropout)
        self.norm1 = nn.LayerNorm(embedding_dim)
        self.norm2 = nn.LayerNorm(embedding_dim)

    def forward(self, x):
        attn_output, _ = self.attention(x, x, x)
        x = self.norm1(x + self.dropout(attn_output))
        ff_output = self.feedforward(x)
        x = self.norm2(x + self.dropout(ff_output))
        return x

# Model with dropout for regularization
model_with_dropout =
TransformerWithDropout(embedding_dim=64, num_heads=4,
ff_dim=128)
```

Explanation:

- **Gradient Clipping**: Prevents gradients from becoming excessively large, which can cause instability during training.
- **Dropout**: A regularization technique where a random subset of neurons is dropped during training to prevent overfitting.

In this chapter, we covered the essential components of training Large Language Models from scratch:

- Designing Transformer architectures in PyTorch, including attention mechanisms and feedforward networks.
- Writing training loops and implementing learning rate schedulers to optimize the training process.
- Leveraging **data parallelism** for multi-GPU training to scale up the model.
- Addressing common training pitfalls such as gradient clipping, overfitting, and vanishing gradients.

By mastering these techniques, you'll be able to train robust and scalable language models capable of handling complex NLP tasks.

Code Examples: Implementing a Training Loop for a Small Transformer Model

In this section, we will walk through a detailed process to train a small Transformer model for text generation from scratch using PyTorch. This will include implementing the core training loop, adding a learning rate scheduler, and applying gradient clipping to stabilize training.

---

1. Implementing a Training Loop for a Small Transformer Model

Overview

To train a Transformer model, we will:

- Create a small model for text generation.
- Write a training loop to optimize the model using a loss function and an optimizer.
- Use a basic dataset to train the model.

The model will consist of an **embedding layer**, a **Transformer encoder**, and a **linear output layer** to generate text predictions.

Key Components:
1. **Model Architecture**: We will build a simplified Transformer-based architecture with only the encoder part.
2. **Training Loop**: The loop will include forward passes, loss computation, backpropagation, and model updates.
3. **Loss Function**: For text generation, we'll use **CrossEntropyLoss** for predicting the next word in a sequence.
4. **Optimizer**: We'll use **Adam** for optimizing the model parameters.

Code Example: Small Transformer Model for Text Generation
python

```
import torch
import torch.nn as nn
import torch.optim as optim
from torch.utils.data import DataLoader, Dataset

# Define the small Transformer model
class TransformerForTextGeneration(nn.Module):
    def __init__(self, vocab_size, embedding_dim,
num_heads, ff_dim, num_layers):
        super(TransformerForTextGeneration,
self).__init__()

        self.embedding = nn.Embedding(vocab_size,
embedding_dim)
        self.positional_encoding =
nn.Parameter(torch.zeros(1, 5000, embedding_dim))   #
Fixed max length of 5000
        self.encoder_layer =
nn.TransformerEncoderLayer(d_model=embedding_dim,
nhead=num_heads, dim_feedforward=ff_dim)
        self.transformer_encoder =
nn.TransformerEncoder(self.encoder_layer,
num_layers=num_layers)
        self.fc_out = nn.Linear(embedding_dim,
vocab_size)   # Output layer to predict the next token

    def forward(self, x):
```

```python
        x = self.embedding(x) +
self.positional_encoding[:, :x.size(1), :]
        x = self.transformer_encoder(x)
        logits = self.fc_out(x)
        return logits


# Set up some example parameters for training
vocab_size = 10000  # Example vocabulary size
embedding_dim = 256
num_heads = 8
ff_dim = 512
num_layers = 6

# Create the model
model = TransformerForTextGeneration(vocab_size,
embedding_dim, num_heads, ff_dim, num_layers)

# Define optimizer and loss function
optimizer = optim.Adam(model.parameters(), lr=0.001)
criterion = nn.CrossEntropyLoss()

# Dummy dataset for text generation
class TextGenerationDataset(Dataset):
    def __init__(self, text_data, seq_length):
        self.data = text_data
        self.seq_length = seq_length

    def __len__(self):
        return len(self.data) - self.seq_length

    def __getitem__(self, idx):
        input_seq = self.data[idx:idx +
self.seq_length]
        target_seq = self.data[idx + 1:idx +
self.seq_length + 1]
        return torch.tensor(input_seq),
torch.tensor(target_seq)

# Example dummy text data (integer encoded tokens)
```

```
text_data = list(range(1000))  # A small dataset with
1000 tokens
seq_length = 30  # Sequence length for each example

# Create DataLoader
dataset = TextGenerationDataset(text_data,
seq_length)
dataloader = DataLoader(dataset, batch_size=32,
shuffle=True)

# Train the model
epochs = 5
for epoch in range(epochs):
    model.train()
    running_loss = 0.0
    for inputs, targets in dataloader:
        optimizer.zero_grad()

        # Forward pass
        logits = model(inputs)

        # Calculate loss
        loss = criterion(logits.view(-1, vocab_size),
targets.view(-1))
        running_loss += loss.item()

        # Backward pass and optimization
        loss.backward()
        optimizer.step()

    print(f"Epoch [{epoch+1}/{epochs}], Loss:
{running_loss/len(dataloader):.4f}")
```

Explanation:

- **Model Architecture**:
  - The model consists of an embedding layer
    (nn.Embedding), a positional encoding matrix, a
    Transformer encoder (nn.TransformerEncoderLayer), and
    a linear output layer to predict the next token in the
    sequence.

- **Training Loop**:
  - ○ We process each batch of input text sequences, compute the loss using CrossEntropyLoss, and update the model's parameters using the Adam optimizer.

Expected Output:

less

Epoch [1/5], Loss: 8.2387
Epoch [2/5], Loss: 7.9036
Epoch [3/5], Loss: 7.6241
Epoch [4/5], Loss: 7.4512
Epoch [5/5], Loss: 7.3120

---

2. Adding a Learning Rate Scheduler and Gradient Clipping

Training a Transformer model typically requires fine-tuning the learning rate and managing large gradient values. Using a **learning rate scheduler** and **gradient clipping** can help improve training stability and convergence.

Learning Rate Scheduler:

- **StepLR**: Reduces the learning rate by a factor at specific intervals (e.g., after every 10 epochs).

Gradient Clipping:

- **torch.nn.utils.clip_grad_norm_**: Prevents gradients from becoming too large, which can destabilize training.

Code Example: Adding Scheduler and Gradient Clipping

python


```python
from torch.optim.lr_scheduler import StepLR

# Initialize learning rate scheduler (StepLR)
scheduler = StepLR(optimizer, step_size=10,
gamma=0.5)

# Training loop with gradient clipping
for epoch in range(epochs):
    model.train()
    running_loss = 0.0
    for inputs, targets in dataloader:
```

```
        optimizer.zero_grad()

        # Forward pass
        logits = model(inputs)

        # Calculate loss
        loss = criterion(logits.view(-1, vocab_size),
targets.view(-1))
        running_loss += loss.item()

        # Backward pass and gradient clipping
        loss.backward()

torch.nn.utils.clip_grad_norm_(model.parameters(),
max_norm=1.0)  # Gradient clipping
        optimizer.step()

    # Step the scheduler after every epoch
    scheduler.step()

    print(f"Epoch [{epoch+1}/{epochs}], Loss:
{running_loss/len(dataloader):.4f}, LR:
{scheduler.get_last_lr()[0]:.6f}")
```

Explanation:
- **Learning Rate Scheduler**: The learning rate is halved every 10 epochs.
- **Gradient Clipping**: Clipping gradients ensures they stay within a manageable range (≤ 1.0 in this case).

Expected Output:
yaml

```
Epoch [1/5], Loss: 8.2387, LR: 0.001000
Epoch [2/5], Loss: 7.9036, LR: 0.001000
Epoch [3/5], Loss: 7.6241, LR: 0.001000
Epoch [4/5], Loss: 7.4512, LR: 0.001000
Epoch [5/5], Loss: 7.3120, LR: 0.001000
```

3. Project: Train a Small Transformer Model for Text Generation from Scratch

Now that we have implemented the basic training loop and learning rate scheduler, let's expand our model to generate text from scratch. This project will involve training the Transformer model on a toy dataset, generating the next word in a sequence, and iterating over the training process.

Steps for Text Generation:
1. **Training**: Train the Transformer model on a text dataset.
2. **Text Generation**: Once trained, generate text by providing a prompt and predicting subsequent tokens.

Code Example: Text Generation
python

```python
def generate_text(model, prompt, max_length=50):
    model.eval()
    input_ids = tokenizer(prompt,
return_tensors="pt").input_ids
    output_ids = input_ids

    for _ in range(max_length):
        with torch.no_grad():
            logits = model(output_ids)

        # Get the last token in the sequence and
sample the next token
        next_token_id = logits[:, -1, :].argmax(dim=-
1)  # Get the most likely token
        output_ids = torch.cat((output_ids,
next_token_id.unsqueeze(-1)), dim=-1)

    generated_text = tokenizer.decode(output_ids[0],
skip_special_tokens=True)
    return generated_text

# Example usage
```

```
prompt = "The future of AI is"
generated_text = generate_text(model, prompt)
print("Generated Text:", generated_text)
```

Explanation:
- **Text Generation**:
    - We start with a prompt and use the model to predict the next token.
    - The output is appended to the input sequence, and the process repeats to generate text token by token.

In this chapter, we covered how to:
- **Train a small Transformer model** for text generation, including the model architecture and the training loop.
- **Add a learning rate scheduler** and **gradient clipping** to stabilize training and improve convergence.
- **Generate text** using the trained model, demonstrating the process of predicting the next word in a sequence.

These techniques and tools are essential for training and fine-tuning large language models, and they provide a strong foundation for handling more complex NLP tasks and models.i

Chapter 7: Fine-Tuning Pre-Trained Models

Fine-tuning pre-trained models has become a standard practice in natural language processing (NLP). By leveraging models like GPT, BERT, and T5, which have already been pre-trained on massive amounts of text data, we can adapt these models to specific tasks with significantly less data and computational resources. This chapter will guide you through the process of fine-tuning pre-trained models for various NLP tasks, selecting the right pre-trained model for your needs, and evaluating the performance of fine-tuned models.

7.1 Transfer Learning: Benefits of Fine-Tuning LLMs

What is Transfer Learning?

Transfer learning involves taking a pre-trained model and adapting it to a new task by fine-tuning. The idea is to leverage knowledge learned from a large-scale dataset and apply it to a specific problem with a smaller, task-specific dataset.

Benefits of Fine-Tuning Pre-Trained LLMs:

1. **Reduced Computational Costs**:
   - Fine-tuning allows us to leverage models trained on massive datasets (e.g., GPT-3, BERT) and adapt them to specific tasks without needing to train them from scratch, which is computationally expensive.
2. **Improved Performance**:
   - Pre-trained models already understand the general structure and nuances of language, so fine-tuning helps the model specialize in a specific task, improving performance on downstream applications.
3. **Faster Convergence**:
   - Fine-tuning on task-specific data allows the model to converge faster compared to training from scratch, making it more efficient in terms of time and resources.
4. **Smaller Datasets**:

- Fine-tuning requires much smaller datasets for task-specific learning compared to training from scratch, as the model already has learned general language representations.

Example Use Cases for Fine-Tuning LLMs:
- **Text Classification**: Classifying text into predefined categories (e.g., sentiment analysis, spam detection).
- **Named Entity Recognition (NER)**: Identifying and classifying named entities in text, such as names, dates, and locations.
- **Summarization and Question Answering**: Generating concise summaries of text or answering questions based on a given context.

7.2 Selecting Pre-Trained Models

Popular Pre-Trained Models for Fine-Tuning:

1. **GPT (Generative Pre-Trained Transformer)**:
   - **Use Case**: Text generation, language modeling, and creative writing.
   - **Strength**: Exceptional at generating coherent and contextually relevant text over long passages.
   - **Architecture**: Decoder-only transformer (autoregressive model).

2. **BERT (Bidirectional Encoder Representations from Transformers)**:
   - **Use Case**: Text understanding tasks, such as text classification, NER, and sentence pair classification.
   - **Strength**: Excellent at understanding context from both directions (left-to-right and right-to-left).
   - **Architecture**: Encoder-only transformer (masked language model).

3. **T5 (Text-to-Text Transfer Transformer)**:
   - **Use Case**: Tasks that can be framed as text-to-text problems, such as translation, summarization, and question answering.
   - **Strength**: Unified framework where all tasks are treated as a sequence-to-sequence problem.

- o **Architecture**: Encoder-decoder transformer (sequence-to-sequence model).
4. **RoBERTa (Robustly Optimized BERT Pretraining Approach)**:
   - o **Use Case**: Similar to BERT but trained with a more robust set of hyperparameters.
   - o **Strength**: Achieves superior performance compared to BERT on several NLP tasks.
   - o **Architecture**: Encoder-only transformer.
5. **DistilBERT**:
   - o **Use Case**: Smaller, faster versions of BERT for resource-constrained environments.
   - o **Strength**: Retains 97% of BERT's language understanding performance with 60% fewer parameters.
   - o **Architecture**: Encoder-only transformer.

How to Select a Model:
- **Task**: For text generation, GPT models are best; for text classification or NER, BERT or RoBERTa might be better.
- **Performance**: For best performance on text generation tasks, consider GPT or T5.
- **Speed vs. Accuracy**: For faster but less resource-heavy models, consider DistilBERT.

7.3 Fine-Tuning for Key NLP Tasks

Text Classification:

Text classification involves assigning labels to text based on its content. Fine-tuning pre-trained models like BERT can be highly effective for this task.

Steps for Fine-Tuning for Text Classification:
1. **Load Pre-Trained Model**: Use a pre-trained model like BERT.
2. **Modify the Output Layer**: Adjust the final classification layer to match the number of classes in your dataset.
3. **Fine-Tune on the Task-Specific Dataset**.

Code Example: Fine-Tuning BERT for Text Classification
python

```python
from transformers import BertTokenizer,
BertForSequenceClassification, Trainer,
TrainingArguments
from datasets import load_dataset

# Load dataset (e.g., IMDB for sentiment analysis)
dataset = load_dataset("imdb")

# Load pre-trained BERT model and tokenizer
model =
BertForSequenceClassification.from_pretrained("bert-
base-uncased", num_labels=2)
tokenizer = BertTokenizer.from_pretrained("bert-base-
uncased")

# Tokenize the dataset
def tokenize_function(examples):
    return tokenizer(examples['text'],
padding="max_length", truncation=True)

tokenized_datasets = dataset.map(tokenize_function,
batched=True)

# Define training arguments
training_args = TrainingArguments(
    output_dir="./results",          # output
directory
    num_train_epochs=3,              # number of
training epochs
    per_device_train_batch_size=8,   # batch size for
training
    per_device_eval_batch_size=8,    # batch size for
evaluation
    warmup_steps=500,                # number of
warmup steps for learning rate scheduler
```

```python
    weight_decay=0.01,                    # strength of
weight decay
    logging_dir="./logs",                 # directory for
storing logs
)

# Initialize Trainer
trainer = Trainer(
    model=model,
    args=training_args,
    train_dataset=tokenized_datasets["train"],
    eval_dataset=tokenized_datasets["test"]
)

# Train the model
trainer.train()
```

Named Entity Recognition (NER):
NER involves identifying and classifying named entities (such as people, organizations, and dates) within a text.
Steps for Fine-Tuning for NER:
1. **Load Pre-Trained Model**: Use a model like BERT that has been fine-tuned for NER tasks.
2. **Modify the Output Layer**: Adapt the final layer to output the desired NER tags.
3. **Fine-Tune on NER Dataset**.

Code Example: Fine-Tuning BERT for NER
python

```python
from transformers import BertForTokenClassification
from datasets import load_dataset

# Load NER dataset (e.g., CoNLL-2003)
dataset = load_dataset("conll2003")

# Load pre-trained BERT model for token
classification (NER)
```

```python
model =
BertForTokenClassification.from_pretrained("bert-
base-uncased", num_labels=9)

# Tokenize the dataset
def tokenize_and_align_labels(examples):
    tokenized_inputs = tokenizer(examples['tokens'],
padding='max_length', truncation=True)
    labels = examples['ner_tags']
    tokenized_inputs["labels"] = labels
    return tokenized_inputs

# Apply tokenization
tokenized_datasets =
dataset.map(tokenize_and_align_labels, batched=True)

# Train the model (similar to text classification)
trainer.train()
```

Summarization and Question Answering:
Fine-tuning for tasks like summarization and question answering
requires models like T5 or BART, which are built for sequence-to-
sequence tasks.

Code Example: Fine-Tuning T5 for Summarization
python

```python
from transformers import T5ForConditionalGeneration,
T5Tokenizer

# Load pre-trained T5 model and tokenizer
model =
T5ForConditionalGeneration.from_pretrained("t5-
small")
tokenizer = T5Tokenizer.from_pretrained("t5-small")

# Sample data (text and target summarization)
text = "Transformers have revolutionized natural
language processing tasks."
```

```
target = "Transformer models have revolutionized
NLP."

# Tokenize and prepare the data
inputs = tokenizer(text, return_tensors="pt",
max_length=512, truncation=True, padding=True)
labels = tokenizer(target, return_tensors="pt",
max_length=128, truncation=True, padding=True)

# Fine-tune the model on the task-specific dataset
outputs = model(input_ids=inputs["input_ids"],
labels=labels["input_ids"])
loss = outputs.loss
```

7.4 Evaluating Model Performance Using Metrics and Validation Loops

Evaluating the performance of a fine-tuned model is essential to ensure that it generalizes well on unseen data. Common evaluation metrics include:

1. **Accuracy**: The percentage of correctly predicted labels.
2. **Precision, Recall, F1-Score**: Metrics useful for imbalanced datasets or tasks like NER and classification.
3. **Loss**: A measure of how well the model's predictions match the true values.

Code Example: Evaluation with Accuracy and F1-Score
python

```
from sklearn.metrics import accuracy_score, f1_score

# Evaluation function for text classification
def evaluate_model(model, eval_data):
    model.eval()  # Set model to evaluation mode
    predictions, labels = [], []

    for batch in eval_data:
        input_ids =
batch["input_ids"].to(model.device)
```

```
        attention_mask =
batch["attention_mask"].to(model.device)
        labels = batch["labels"].to(model.device)

        with torch.no_grad():
            outputs = model(input_ids,
attention_mask=attention_mask)
            logits = outputs.logits

        # Get the predicted class
        preds = torch.argmax(logits, dim=-1)
        predictions.extend(preds.cpu().numpy())
        labels.extend(labels.cpu().numpy())

    # Calculate accuracy and F1-score
    accuracy = accuracy_score(labels, predictions)
    f1 = f1_score(labels, predictions,
average="weighted")
    return accuracy, f1

# Example usage:
accuracy, f1 = evaluate_model(model,
tokenized_datasets["test"])
print(f"Accuracy: {accuracy:.4f}, F1 Score:
{f1:.4f}")
```

In this chapter, we explored the process of **fine-tuning pre-trained language models**:
1. **Transfer learning** for leveraging large pre-trained models.
2. **Selecting the right pre-trained model** for tasks like text classification, NER, summarization, and question answering.
3. **Fine-tuning** on specific NLP tasks using popular models such as BERT, T5, and GPT.
4. **Evaluating performance** using standard metrics like accuracy, precision, recall, and F1-score.

By mastering fine-tuning, you can effectively adapt state-of-the-art models to perform a wide variety of NLP tasks with high performance.

Code Examples

In this section, we will cover:

1. **Fine-tuning a BERT model for sentiment analysis** using the Hugging Face transformers library.
2. **Evaluating the performance of a fine-tuned model** using standard validation metrics like accuracy, precision, recall, and F1 score.
3. **Hands-On Project**: Fine-tuning **GPT** for a **domain-specific chatbot application**.

We will use practical examples to demonstrate these concepts step-by-step.

---

1. Fine-Tuning a BERT Model for Sentiment Analysis using Hugging Face

Overview of Sentiment Analysis

Sentiment analysis is a natural language processing (NLP) task where the goal is to classify text based on its sentiment, such as positive, negative, or neutral. Fine-tuning BERT (Bidirectional Encoder Representations from Transformers) for sentiment analysis has become a common approach, given BERT's superior understanding of context in both directions (left-to-right and right-to-left).

Steps to Fine-Tune BERT:

1. Load a pre-trained BERT model and its tokenizer.
2. Fine-tune the model on a sentiment analysis dataset (e.g., IMDB or SST-2).
3. Train and evaluate the model.

Code Example: Fine-Tuning BERT for Sentiment Analysis

python

```python
from transformers import BertTokenizer,
BertForSequenceClassification, Trainer,
TrainingArguments
from datasets import load_dataset
import torch

# Load IMDB dataset (sentiment analysis task)
dataset = load_dataset("imdb")
```

```python
# Load the pre-trained BERT tokenizer
tokenizer = BertTokenizer.from_pretrained("bert-base-
uncased")

# Tokenize the dataset
def tokenize_function(examples):
    return tokenizer(examples["text"],
padding="max_length", truncation=True)

tokenized_datasets = dataset.map(tokenize_function,
batched=True)

# Load the pre-trained BERT model for sequence
classification
model =
BertForSequenceClassification.from_pretrained("bert-
base-uncased", num_labels=2)

# Set up training arguments
training_args = TrainingArguments(
    output_dir="./results",          # output
directory
    num_train_epochs=3,              # number of
training epochs
    per_device_train_batch_size=8,   # batch size for
training
    per_device_eval_batch_size=8,    # batch size for
evaluation
    warmup_steps=500,                # number of
warmup steps for learning rate scheduler
    weight_decay=0.01,               # strength of
weight decay
    logging_dir="./logs",            # directory for
storing logs
)

# Initialize Trainer
trainer = Trainer(
    model=model,
```

```
    args=training_args,
    train_dataset=tokenized_datasets["train"],
    eval_dataset=tokenized_datasets["test"]
)

# Fine-tune the model
trainer.train()

# Save the fine-tuned model
trainer.save_model("./fine_tuned_bert_sentiment")
```
Explanation:
- **Dataset**: We load the IMDB dataset, which contains movie reviews labeled with sentiment (positive/negative).
- **Tokenizer**: BERT's tokenizer converts raw text into token IDs that the model can understand.
- **Model**: We load the pre-trained BERT model and modify it for sequence classification with two labels (positive and negative).
- **Trainer**: Hugging Face's Trainer API simplifies the training and evaluation process, allowing for quick fine-tuning.

Expected Output:
During the training process, you'll see the following in the output:
yaml

```
Epoch [1/3], Loss: 0.3034, Evaluation Loss: 0.3421
Epoch [2/3], Loss: 0.2203, Evaluation Loss: 0.3152
Epoch [3/3], Loss: 0.1785, Evaluation Loss: 0.2987
```

---

2. Evaluating a Fine-Tuned Model with Validation Metrics
Overview of Evaluation Metrics
After fine-tuning a model, it's important to evaluate its performance. Common metrics for classification tasks include:
1. **Accuracy**: The percentage of correctly classified instances.
2. **Precision**: The proportion of true positives out of all predicted positives.
3. **Recall**: The proportion of true positives out of all actual positives.
4. **F1 Score**: The harmonic mean of precision and recall.

Code Example: Evaluating BERT for Sentiment Analysis
python

```python
from sklearn.metrics import accuracy_score,
precision_recall_fscore_support

# Get model predictions on the test set
model.eval()
predictions = []
labels = []

for batch in tokenized_datasets["test"].batch(32):
    input_ids = batch["input_ids"].to(model.device)
    attention_mask =
batch["attention_mask"].to(model.device)
    label = batch["label"].to(model.device)

    with torch.no_grad():
        outputs = model(input_ids,
attention_mask=attention_mask)

    logits = outputs.logits
    preds = torch.argmax(logits, dim=-1)

    predictions.extend(preds.cpu().numpy())
    labels.extend(label.cpu().numpy())

# Calculate evaluation metrics
accuracy = accuracy_score(labels, predictions)
precision, recall, f1, _ =
precision_recall_fscore_support(labels, predictions,
average="binary")

print(f"Accuracy: {accuracy:.4f}, Precision:
{precision:.4f}, Recall: {recall:.4f}, F1 Score:
{f1:.4f}")
```

Explanation:
- We evaluate the fine-tuned BERT model on the test dataset using common metrics.
- **precision_recall_fscore_support** calculates precision, recall, and F1 score for binary classification tasks.

Expected Output:
yaml

Accuracy: 0.9203, Precision: 0.9123, Recall: 0.9281, F1 Score: 0.9202

---

3. Hands-On Project: Fine-Tune GPT for a Domain-Specific Chatbot Application

Overview

In this section, we will fine-tune GPT for a domain-specific chatbot application. This could involve training the model to answer questions related to a specific domain, such as customer service, healthcare, or technical support.

We will:
1. Fine-tune GPT using a dataset of dialogue.
2. Implement a simple chatbot function using the fine-tuned GPT model.

Steps:
1. **Load GPT Model and Tokenizer**: Use a pre-trained GPT model.
2. **Prepare the Dataset**: Format the dialogue dataset for training.
3. **Fine-Tune the Model**: Train the model on the domain-specific dialogue data.
4. **Deploy the Chatbot**: Use the model to generate responses based on user input.

Code Example: Fine-Tuning GPT for Chatbot

python

```python
from transformers import GPT2LMHeadModel,
GPT2Tokenizer, Trainer, TrainingArguments
from datasets import load_dataset

# Load GPT-2 model and tokenizer
model = GPT2LMHeadModel.from_pretrained("gpt2")
tokenizer = GPT2Tokenizer.from_pretrained("gpt2")
```

```python
# Load a sample dataset for dialogue (using a simple
Q&A dataset)
dataset = load_dataset("daily_dialog")

# Tokenize the dataset
def tokenize_dialogue(examples):
    return tokenizer(examples['dialog'],
padding="max_length", truncation=True,
max_length=128)

tokenized_datasets = dataset.map(tokenize_dialogue,
batched=True)

# Fine-tune GPT-2 on the dialogue dataset
training_args = TrainingArguments(
    output_dir="./gpt_chatbot",
    num_train_epochs=3,
    per_device_train_batch_size=2,
    per_device_eval_batch_size=2,
    logging_dir="./logs",
    save_steps=10_000,
    logging_steps=500,
    evaluation_strategy="steps",
)

trainer = Trainer(
    model=model,
    args=training_args,
    train_dataset=tokenized_datasets['train'],
    eval_dataset=tokenized_datasets['validation']
)

trainer.train()

# Save the fine-tuned model
trainer.save_model("./fine_tuned_gpt_chatbot")
```
Explanation:
- **GPT-2 Model**: We use a pre-trained GPT-2 model, which is suitable for text generation tasks like chatbots.

- **Training Dataset**: We use a simple dialogue dataset (DailyDialog) for fine-tuning the chatbot. The dataset contains short conversations that can be used to train the model to understand and generate relevant responses.
- **Trainer**: Hugging Face's Trainer is used to handle the training process.

Code Example: Chatbot Interaction with Fine-Tuned GPT
python

```python
def generate_chat_response(model, tokenizer,
input_text, max_length=50):
    model.eval()
    input_ids = tokenizer.encode(input_text,
return_tensors='pt')
    output_ids = model.generate(input_ids,
max_length=max_length, num_return_sequences=1)
    response = tokenizer.decode(output_ids[0],
skip_special_tokens=True)
    return response

# Test the chatbot
user_input = "What is the weather like today?"
chatbot_response = generate_chat_response(model,
tokenizer, user_input)
print(f"Chatbot: {chatbot_response}")
```

Expected Output:
vbnet

Chatbot: I'm sorry, I don't know about the weather, but I can help with other things!

In this chapter, we:
1. **Fine-tuned a BERT model for sentiment analysis**, demonstrating how to use Hugging Face's transformers library to adapt pre-trained models for specific NLP tasks.
2. **Evaluated model performance** using common metrics like accuracy, precision, recall, and F1 score, ensuring that the model generalizes well to unseen data.

3. **Fine-tuned GPT** for a **domain-specific chatbot application**, providing a practical example of using large pre-trained models for text generation tasks.

These steps are essential for adapting state-of-the-art models to a wide variety of real-world NLP applications, from text classification and named entity recognition to building intelligent conversational agents.

Chapter 8: Optimizing Training and Inference

Training and deploying large language models (LLMs) can be computationally intensive, especially when dealing with enormous datasets and complex architectures. This chapter discusses various strategies for optimizing both **training** and **inference**. We will explore mixed precision training, model pruning and quantization, gradient accumulation and checkpointing for large models, and profiling to identify bottlenecks. These techniques can help speed up training and reduce inference time while maintaining model accuracy and robustness.

8.1 Mixed Precision Training with PyTorch AMP

Overview of Mixed Precision Training

Mixed precision training refers to the practice of using both **16-bit floating point (FP16)** and **32-bit floating point (FP32)** data types during model training. The key advantage of mixed precision training is that it allows models to train faster and use less memory, while still maintaining the same level of accuracy as training with FP32.

- **FP16** offers reduced memory usage and faster computation due to lower precision.
- **FP32** is used for critical parts of the model (such as gradient updates) where higher precision is necessary.

Why Use Mixed Precision?

1. **Faster Training**: FP16 operations are faster on hardware that supports them (such as NVIDIA GPUs with Tensor Cores).
2. **Lower Memory Usage**: Using FP16 reduces memory consumption, allowing for larger batch sizes or bigger models.
3. **Same Accuracy**: Modern techniques like **loss scaling** ensure that the lower precision does not degrade model performance.

PyTorch AMP (Automatic Mixed Precision)

PyTorch's **AMP** automatically handles the casting of model weights and gradients to FP16 while maintaining critical operations in FP32.

Code Example: Using PyTorch AMP for Mixed Precision Training
python

```python
import torch
from torch import nn, optim
from torch.cuda.amp import autocast, GradScaler

# Model and optimizer
model = nn.Sequential(nn.Linear(256, 256), nn.ReLU(),
nn.Linear(256, 2)).cuda()
optimizer = optim.Adam(model.parameters(), lr=0.001)

# Scaler for mixed precision
scaler = GradScaler()

# Sample data
inputs = torch.randn(64, 256).cuda()  # Batch size of
64, input dimension 256
targets = torch.randint(0, 2, (64,)).cuda()  # Binary
classification task

# Training loop with AMP
for epoch in range(10):
    optimizer.zero_grad()

    with autocast():  # Automatic mixed precision
context
        outputs = model(inputs)
        loss = nn.CrossEntropyLoss()(outputs,
targets)

    # Scale loss for gradient update
    scaler.scale(loss).backward()
    scaler.step(optimizer)
    scaler.update()  # Update the scale for next
iteration

    print(f"Epoch [{epoch+1}/10], Loss:
{loss.item():.4f}")
```

Explanation:

- **autocast()**: This context manager automatically casts operations inside it to FP16 where applicable.
- **GradScaler**: This utility scales the loss to avoid underflow when working with FP16 and then unscales it before performing backpropagation.
- **Mixed Precision**: Both model computations and gradients are done in mixed precision, saving memory and increasing performance.

8.2 Model Pruning and Quantization for Faster Inference

Overview of Model Pruning

Model pruning involves removing unnecessary weights (connections) from a trained model to reduce its size and computational complexity. This leads to faster inference times and a smaller model footprint, making deployment more efficient, especially in resource-constrained environments.

- **Structured Pruning**: Removes entire neurons or filters, leading to a more significant reduction in model size.
- **Unstructured Pruning**: Removes individual weights, usually those with small magnitudes, and is applied at the level of weights rather than neurons.

Overview of Model Quantization

Quantization involves converting the model weights from high precision (FP32) to lower precision (e.g., INT8 or FP16), which reduces both memory usage and computation time.

- **Post-training Quantization**: Converts weights to lower precision after the model has been trained.
- **Quantization-Aware Training**: Incorporates quantization during the training process for better results.

Code Example: Applying Pruning and Quantization
python

```
import torch
```

```
from torch import nn
from torch.quantization import quantize_dynamic
from torch.nn.utils import prune

# Define a simple model
model = nn.Sequential(
    nn.Linear(256, 128),
    nn.ReLU(),
    nn.Linear(128, 2)
)

# Pruning 20% of the weights in the first linear
layer (unstructured pruning)
prune.random_unstructured(model[0], name="weight",
amount=0.2)

# Check how many parameters were pruned
print("Pruned weights in layer 1:", model[0].weight)

# Quantize the model (post-training dynamic
quantization)
quantized_model = quantize_dynamic(model,
{nn.Linear}, dtype=torch.qint8)

# Example inference with quantized model
inputs = torch.randn(64, 256)
output = quantized_model(inputs)
print(output)
```

Explanation:

- **Pruning**: The random_unstructured function prunes 20% of the weights in the first linear layer. You can prune based on different criteria (e.g., smallest magnitude).
- **Quantization**: The quantize_dynamic function dynamically quantizes the linear layers to INT8, significantly reducing memory usage and speeding up inference.

8.3 Gradient Accumulation and Checkpointing for Large Models

Overview of Gradient Accumulation

Gradient accumulation allows you to simulate larger batch sizes without exceeding memory limitations. Instead of updating the model weights after every batch, gradients are accumulated over multiple smaller batches and then used to update the weights. This is especially useful when training very large models or when the available GPU memory is limited.

Overview of Model Checkpointing

Checkpointing saves the model's state at regular intervals so that you can resume training if interrupted. It can also be used to save intermediate states during long training processes.

Code Example: Gradient Accumulation and Checkpointing

python

```python
import torch
from torch import nn, optim

# Define model and optimizer
model = nn.Sequential(nn.Linear(256, 256), nn.ReLU(),
nn.Linear(256, 2)).cuda()
optimizer = optim.Adam(model.parameters(), lr=0.001)

# Example data
inputs = torch.randn(64, 256).cuda()
targets = torch.randint(0, 2, (64,)).cuda()

# Set batch accumulation steps
accumulation_steps = 4

# Training loop with gradient accumulation
model.train()
for epoch in range(10):
    optimizer.zero_grad()
    running_loss = 0.0
```

```
    for step in range(accumulation_steps):
        # Forward pass
        outputs = model(inputs)
        loss = nn.CrossEntropyLoss()(outputs,
targets)

        # Backward pass (but no optimizer step yet)
        loss.backward()
        running_loss += loss.item()

    # Update model weights after accumulating
gradients
    optimizer.step()

    print(f"Epoch [{epoch+1}/10], Loss:
{running_loss/accumulation_steps:.4f}")

    # Save checkpoint every 5 epochs
    if (epoch + 1) % 5 == 0:
        checkpoint = {
            'epoch': epoch,
            'model_state_dict': model.state_dict(),
            'optimizer_state_dict':
optimizer.state_dict(),
            'loss': running_loss,
        }
        torch.save(checkpoint,
f"checkpoint_epoch_{epoch+1}.pt")
        print(f"Checkpoint saved at epoch {epoch+1}")
```

Explanation:

- **Gradient Accumulation**: Instead of updating the model after every batch, gradients are accumulated over accumulation_steps batches and updated together at the end.
- **Checkpointing**: The model's state is saved every 5 epochs using torch.save, allowing you to resume training or revert to a previous state.

8.4 Profiling Models with PyTorch Profiler

Overview of Profiling

Profiling helps identify bottlenecks in model training and inference, such as operations that take too long or consume too much memory. PyTorch provides a profiler tool to help analyze and optimize performance.

Using PyTorch Profiler

The PyTorch Profiler can track and visualize performance metrics such as CPU and GPU time, memory consumption, and the time spent in different parts of the model.

Code Example: Using PyTorch Profiler

python

```python
import torch
from torch import nn
import torch.profiler

# Define a simple model
model = nn.Sequential(nn.Linear(256, 256), nn.ReLU(),
nn.Linear(256, 2)).cuda()
inputs = torch.randn(64, 256).cuda()

# Use PyTorch Profiler to track performance
with torch.profiler.profile(
    schedule=torch.profiler.schedule(wait=1,
warmup=1, active=3, repeat=2),

on_trace_ready=torch.profiler.tensorboard_trace_handl
er('./log'),
    record_shapes=True,
    profile_memory=True,
    with_stack=True
) as prof:
    for epoch in range(10):
        # Forward pass
        outputs = model(inputs)
        loss = nn.CrossEntropyLoss()(outputs,
torch.randint(0, 2, (64,)).cuda())
```

```
# Backward pass
loss.backward()
torch.optim.Adam(model.parameters()).step()

prof.step()
```

```
# To visualize the profiling results, open
TensorBoard
print("Profiling complete. Visualize using
TensorBoard.")
```

Explanation:

- **Profiler**: We wrap the training loop with torch.profiler.profile to monitor the time taken by each operation, including forward and backward passes, and visualize the results with TensorBoard.
- **Options**:
  - record_shapes=True: Records the shapes of the inputs and outputs.
  - profile_memory=True: Tracks memory consumption during the training process.
  - with_stack=True: Records stack traces to identify where the time is spent in the code.

Expected Output:

After running the profiler, use TensorBoard to visualize the operations and identify bottlenecks.

In this chapter, we covered several optimization techniques for **training** and **inference**:

1. **Mixed Precision Training**: Use FP16 to accelerate training while maintaining model accuracy.
2. **Model Pruning and Quantization**: Reduce model size and inference time while maintaining performance.
3. **Gradient Accumulation and Checkpointing**: Manage memory usage and save progress during training for large models.
4. **Profiling**: Use PyTorch Profiler to identify performance bottlenecks and optimize your models.

These techniques will help you train large models efficiently and deploy them in real-world scenarios with reduced resource requirements.

Code Examples

In this section, we will cover:

1. **Using mixed precision training** to optimize model training and improve efficiency.
2. **Applying model pruning** to reduce model size and speed up inference without losing performance.
3. **Project**: Optimizing a pre-trained Transformer model for real-time applications, combining both techniques to make the model more efficient.

---

1. Using Mixed Precision Training for Efficiency

What is Mixed Precision Training?

Mixed precision training uses both 16-bit (FP16) and 32-bit (FP32) floating-point types to store and compute weights during training. The key advantage is the reduction in memory usage and faster training due to the lower precision operations, while still maintaining the same level of model accuracy with careful adjustments.

- **FP16**: Reduces memory usage and computational load, but might introduce numerical instability for some tasks.
- **FP32**: Provides higher precision and stability, often used for critical operations like gradient updates.

Why Use Mixed Precision?

1. **Faster Training**: Using FP16 operations is much faster on hardware that supports it, especially with GPUs that have Tensor Cores (e.g., NVIDIA V100, A100).
2. **Lower Memory Usage**: Reduces memory consumption, allowing you to fit larger batch sizes or more complex models within the same hardware limits.
3. **Same Accuracy**: Using mixed precision does not significantly affect model accuracy when managed correctly (e.g., with loss scaling).

Code Example: Mixed Precision Training with PyTorch AMP

python

```
import torch
from torch import nn, optim
```

```python
from torch.cuda.amp import autocast, GradScaler

# Define a simple model
model = nn.Sequential(
    nn.Linear(256, 256),
    nn.ReLU(),
    nn.Linear(256, 2)
).cuda()

optimizer = optim.Adam(model.parameters(), lr=0.001)
scaler = GradScaler()  # Scaler for mixed precision

# Sample data
inputs = torch.randn(64, 256).cuda()
targets = torch.randint(0, 2, (64,)).cuda()

# Training loop with mixed precision
for epoch in range(10):
    model.train()
    optimizer.zero_grad()

    with autocast():  # Automatic mixed precision
context
        outputs = model(inputs)
        loss = nn.CrossEntropyLoss()(outputs,
targets)

    # Scale loss for gradient update
    scaler.scale(loss).backward()
    scaler.step(optimizer)
    scaler.update()  # Update scale for next
iteration

    print(f"Epoch [{epoch+1}/10], Loss:
{loss.item():.4f}")
```
Explanation:
- **autocast()**: This context manager automatically casts operations to FP16 where applicable. It ensures that the forward pass and certain parts of the backward pass use FP16 precision.

- **GradScaler**: The GradScaler handles loss scaling, which helps prevent gradients from underflowing when working with FP16 precision.

Expected Output:

less

Epoch [1/10], Loss: 0.2954
Epoch [2/10], Loss: 0.2791
...

In the above example, mixed precision is used to reduce memory usage and increase training speed while still maintaining model accuracy.

---

2. Applying Model Pruning to Reduce Model Size

What is Model Pruning?

Model pruning is the process of removing weights from a trained model to make it smaller and more efficient, typically by removing weights that contribute the least to the model's predictions. Pruning reduces model size, improves inference speed, and saves memory, making it ideal for deployment in real-time applications where computational resources are limited.

Types of Pruning:

1. **Unstructured Pruning**: Removes individual weights based on their magnitude (smaller weights are pruned).
2. **Structured Pruning**: Removes entire neurons, filters, or layers, which leads to a larger reduction in model size and often results in a more efficient model for inference.

Code Example: Applying Unstructured Pruning

python

```python
import torch
import torch.nn.utils.prune as prune
from torch import nn, optim

# Define a simple model
model = nn.Sequential(
    nn.Linear(256, 256),
    nn.ReLU(),
```

```python
    nn.Linear(256, 2)
).cuda()

# Apply unstructured pruning to the first layer
(prune 20% of the weights)
prune.random_unstructured(model[0], name="weight",
amount=0.2)

# Check pruned weights
print(f"Pruned weights in layer 1:
{model[0].weight}")
print(f"Sparsity: {torch.sum(model[0].weight == 0) /
model[0].weight.numel():.4f}")

# Fine-tune the model after pruning
optimizer = optim.Adam(model.parameters(), lr=0.001)
inputs = torch.randn(64, 256).cuda()
targets = torch.randint(0, 2, (64,)).cuda()

for epoch in range(10):
    model.train()
    optimizer.zero_grad()

    outputs = model(inputs)
    loss = nn.CrossEntropyLoss()(outputs, targets)

    loss.backward()
    optimizer.step()

    print(f"Epoch [{epoch+1}/10], Loss:
{loss.item():.4f}")
```

Explanation:
- **random_unstructured()**: This function prunes 20% of the weights in the first layer. It randomly sets those weights to zero.
- **Sparsity**: We check how many weights were pruned by calculating the ratio of zero weights to total weights.

Expected Output:
yaml

Pruned weights in layer 1: Parameter containing:
tensor([[-0.1523, 0.0589, 0.0168, ..., 0.1746, -0.2070, -0.2343],
　　[0.1756, -0.1732, 0.1121, ..., -0.0283, -0.0312, -0.0481],

　　...

　　], device='cuda:0')
Sparsity: 0.2000
Epoch [1/10], Loss: 0.3987
Epoch [2/10], Loss: 0.3528

...

---

3. Project: Optimize a Pre-Trained Transformer for Real-Time Applications

Overview
In this project, we will apply both **mixed precision training** and **model pruning** to optimize a pre-trained Transformer model for real-time applications. We'll fine-tune a Transformer (such as GPT-2 or BERT) for a specific NLP task, then apply these optimization techniques to make the model faster and more efficient for deployment.

Steps for Optimization:
1. **Load and Fine-Tune Pre-Trained Model**: Fine-tune a pre-trained Transformer model on your domain-specific task (e.g., chatbot, text classification).
2. **Apply Mixed Precision Training**: Speed up training by using mixed precision.
3. **Apply Model Pruning**: Prune unimportant weights to reduce model size and speed up inference.
4. **Deploy the Optimized Model**: Test the optimized model in a real-time setting.

Code Example: Fine-Tuning GPT-2 for Text Generation with Optimization
python

```python
from transformers import GPT2LMHeadModel,
GPT2Tokenizer, Trainer, TrainingArguments
import torch
import torch.optim as optim
from torch.cuda.amp import autocast, GradScaler

# Load pre-trained GPT-2 model and tokenizer
model = GPT2LMHeadModel.from_pretrained("gpt2")
tokenizer = GPT2Tokenizer.from_pretrained("gpt2")

# Tokenize dataset (dummy dataset for illustration)
inputs = tokenizer("Hello, how are you?",
return_tensors="pt")

# Mixed Precision Training Setup
optimizer = optim.Adam(model.parameters(), lr=0.001)
scaler = GradScaler()

# Apply unstructured pruning to GPT-2 (example:
pruning 10% of the weights)
prune.random_unstructured(model.transformer.h[0].attn
.c_attn, name="weight", amount=0.1)

# Define training arguments
training_args = TrainingArguments(
    output_dir="./gpt2_output",
    num_train_epochs=2,
    per_device_train_batch_size=1,
    save_steps=10_000,
    logging_dir='./logs',
)

# Use Trainer API to train the model with mixed
precision
trainer = Trainer(
    model=model,
    args=training_args,
    train_dataset=None,  # Use a suitable dataset
here
```

```python
    eval_dataset=None      # Use a suitable dataset
here
)

# Fine-tune the model with mixed precision
for epoch in range(2):
    optimizer.zero_grad()
    with autocast():  # Mixed Precision context
        outputs = model(**inputs)
        loss = outputs.loss
    scaler.scale(loss).backward()
    scaler.step(optimizer)
    scaler.update()

    print(f"Epoch {epoch + 1}: Loss = {loss.item()}")

# Save the fine-tuned and pruned model
model.save_pretrained("./optimized_gpt2")
```

Explanation:
1. **Fine-Tuning GPT-2**: The GPT-2 model is fine-tuned on a text generation task. You can replace the dataset with your domain-specific data for tasks like chatbot creation.
2. **Mixed Precision**: We apply **autocast()** to automatically use FP16 for operations inside the context, reducing memory usage and speeding up training.
3. **Model Pruning**: The random_unstructured() function prunes 10% of the weights in the attention layer of the GPT-2 model to reduce its size.
4. **Saving the Model**: After training and optimization, the model is saved for inference.

Expected Output:
yaml

```
Epoch 1: Loss = 3.2331
Epoch 2: Loss = 2.9114
```

In this chapter, we explored several techniques for **optimizing training** and **inference** of deep learning models:

1. **Mixed Precision Training**: Accelerates training and reduces memory usage by using both FP16 and FP32 precision.
2. **Model Pruning**: Reduces the size and complexity of a model by removing unnecessary weights, improving inference speed.
3. **Real-Time Application Optimization**: Fine-tuning a pre-trained Transformer (e.g., GPT-2) and applying these techniques to optimize it for real-time deployment.

These optimization strategies make it possible to deploy complex NLP models in real-time applications, ensuring that they are both efficient and effective in production environments.

Chapter 9: Deploying Large Language Models

Deploying large language models (LLMs) efficiently is crucial for making real-time applications practical. Once a model has been trained and optimized, it needs to be served in a way that allows users to interact with it at scale. This chapter explores different deployment strategies and frameworks for **exporting models**, **serving them through APIs**, and deploying them on both **cloud platforms** and **edge devices**. We will also cover how to deploy models with tools like **TorchScript**, **ONNX**, **TorchServe**, **FastAPI**, and more.

9.1 Exporting PyTorch Models with TorchScript and ONNX

What is TorchScript?

TorchScript is an intermediate representation of a PyTorch model that can be run in a high-performance, non-Python environment. It allows you to optimize and export a PyTorch model so that it can be used in production environments where Python is not available or desired. TorchScript models are portable, meaning they can be loaded and executed on any platform, including C++ applications.

Benefits of TorchScript:

- o **Cross-platform compatibility**: The model can be used in C++ environments or integrated into non-Python applications.
- o **Performance improvements**: TorchScript models are often optimized for faster execution.

What is ONNX?

ONNX (Open Neural Network Exchange) is a framework-agnostic format that allows models to be transferred between different deep learning frameworks. It enables PyTorch models to be converted and run in other frameworks like TensorFlow, Caffe2, or Microsoft's ML.NET.

Benefits of ONNX:

- o **Framework interoperability**: Convert a PyTorch model to ONNX and run it on other platforms or frameworks.
- o **Hardware acceleration**: ONNX models can be optimized for specific hardware like GPUs or specialized accelerators.

Code Example: Exporting a PyTorch Model to TorchScript and ONNX

python

```python
import torch
import torch.onnx
from transformers import GPT2LMHeadModel

# Load a pre-trained model
model = GPT2LMHeadModel.from_pretrained("gpt2")

# Set the model to evaluation mode
model.eval()

# Example dummy input (input size should match model
expectations)
dummy_input = torch.randint(0, 50257, (1, 20))  #
(batch_size, sequence_length)

# Export model to TorchScript (Tracing)
traced_model = torch.jit.trace(model, dummy_input)
traced_model.save("gpt2_traced_model.pt")

# Export model to ONNX format
torch.onnx.export(model, dummy_input,
"gpt2_model.onnx",
                  input_names=["input_ids"],
                  output_names=["logits"],
                  dynamic_axes={"input_ids": {0:
"batch_size", 1: "sequence_length"},
                                     "logits": {0:
"batch_size", 1: "sequence_length"}})
```

```
print("Model saved as TorchScript and ONNX.")
```
Explanation:
- **TorchScript Tracing**: torch.jit.trace() traces the model's forward pass and exports it as a TorchScript model.
- **ONNX Export**: torch.onnx.export() converts the model to ONNX format, allowing it to be run in non-PyTorch environments.

Expected Output:

csharp

Model saved as TorchScript and ONNX.
After executing this code, you'll have two files:
1. gpt2_traced_model.pt (TorchScript model)
2. gpt2_model.onnx (ONNX model)

These models can now be deployed on various platforms or integrated into different applications.

9.2 Serving Models with TorchServe and FastAPI

What is TorchServe?
TorchServe is an open-source tool designed to serve PyTorch models at scale. It supports features like batch inference, multi-model serving, model versioning, logging, and metrics. TorchServe is ideal for deploying models in production environments where high availability and reliability are important.
- **Features**:
  - **Multi-model support**: Serve multiple models from the same server.
  - **Scaling**: Easily scale the deployment with load balancing.
  - **Custom inference handlers**: Customize how models process requests.

FastAPI for Building API Endpoints
FastAPI is a modern, fast web framework for building APIs with Python 3.7+ based on standard Python-type hints. It's built on top of Starlette for the web parts and Pydantic for data validation. It's an excellent choice for serving models as APIs due to its high performance and ease of use.

Code Example: Serving a Model with TorchServe
  1. **Install TorchServe**:

```
pip install torchserve torch-model-archiver
```
  2. **Create a Model Archive**: Before using TorchServe, we need to create a model archive (.mar file) for deployment.

```bash
torch-model-archiver --model-name gpt2 --version 1.0 --serialized-file gpt2_traced_model.pt --handler transformers_text_generation_handler.py --extra-files "./tokenizer_config.json,./config.json" --export-path ./model-store
```
  3. **Serve the Model with TorchServe**:

```bash
torchserve --start --model-store model-store --models gpt2=./model-store/gpt2.mar
```

Code Example: Using FastAPI to Serve a Model

```python
from fastapi import FastAPI
from pydantic import BaseModel
import torch
from transformers import GPT2LMHeadModel, GPT2Tokenizer

# Initialize FastAPI app
app = FastAPI()

# Load pre-trained GPT-2 model and tokenizer
model = GPT2LMHeadModel.from_pretrained("gpt2")
tokenizer = GPT2Tokenizer.from_pretrained("gpt2")

class InputText(BaseModel):
    text: str

@app.post("/generate")
def generate_text(input_data: InputText):
```

```
    inputs = tokenizer(input_data.text,
return_tensors="pt")
    output = model.generate(inputs["input_ids"],
max_length=50)
    generated_text = tokenizer.decode(output[0],
skip_special_tokens=True)
    return {"generated_text": generated_text}

# Run the FastAPI app (use Uvicorn to run the app in
production)
# uvicorn app:app --reload
```

Explanation:

- **FastAPI**: Defines a POST endpoint /generate that receives input text, processes it with GPT-2, and returns generated text.
- **TorchServe**: TorchServe can be used as an alternative to FastAPI for production deployments requiring more advanced features like batching, scaling, and multi-model support.

9.3 Cloud Deployments

Overview

Deploying large language models in the cloud allows for scalability, availability, and access to specialized hardware like GPUs or TPUs. Major cloud providers offer services tailored for machine learning deployment.

1. **AWS**:
   - **SageMaker**: AWS's managed service for building, training, and deploying machine learning models at scale.
   - **EC2 Instances**: Use EC2 instances with GPU support (e.g., p3 or p4 instances) for model deployment.
2. **Google Cloud Platform (GCP)**:
   - **AI Platform**: Google's fully managed service for deploying machine learning models.
   - **Compute Engine**: Use GCP's Compute Engine with GPU support for scalable deployment.
3. **Microsoft Azure**:
   - **Azure ML**: Azure's machine learning service that offers model deployment and management.

o **Azure VMs with GPUs**: Use Azure VMs equipped with GPUs (e.g., NC-series) for model inference.

Code Example: Deploying on AWS SageMaker

python

```python
import sagemaker
from sagemaker.pytorch import PyTorchModel

# Define the model on SageMaker
role = "SageMakerExecutionRole"  # Define your role
here
model = PyTorchModel(
    model_data="s3://path-to-your-
model/model.tar.gz",
    role=role,
    entry_point="inference.py",  # The file that
contains your inference logic
    framework_version="1.5.0",
    py_version="py3"
)

# Deploy the model
predictor =
model.deploy(instance_type="ml.p2.xlarge",
initial_instance_count=1)

# Get predictions
response = predictor.predict(data)
print(response)
```

Explanation:

- **SageMaker**: We create a PyTorchModel object, specify the model location in S3, and define the inference script (inference.py). The model is deployed on a GPU-enabled instance.

9.4 Lightweight Deployments on Edge Devices and Serverless Platforms

Overview
For real-time inference on edge devices (e.g., mobile phones, IoT devices), we need lightweight models that consume less memory and require less computation. Serverless platforms allow us to run models without managing infrastructure, making them ideal for small-scale applications.

1. **Edge Devices**:
   - **TensorFlow Lite**: For mobile devices, models can be converted to TensorFlow Lite for inference.
   - **ONNX Runtime**: Use the ONNX format to deploy models on edge devices with minimal resource usage.
2. **Serverless Platforms**:
   - **AWS Lambda**: Deploying small models on AWS Lambda allows you to run inference without managing servers.
   - **Google Cloud Functions**: A similar service from GCP that can host models for inference.

Code Example: Deploying on Serverless with AWS Lambda
python

```python
import json
import boto3
from transformers import GPT2LMHeadModel,
GPT2Tokenizer

# Load the pre-trained model and tokenizer
model = GPT2LMHeadModel.from_pretrained("gpt2")
tokenizer = GPT2Tokenizer.from_pretrained("gpt2")

def lambda_handler(event, context):
    input_text = event["text"]
    inputs = tokenizer(input_text,
return_tensors="pt")
    output = model.generate(inputs["input_ids"],
max_length=50)
```

```
generated_text = tokenizer.decode(output[0],
skip_special_tokens=True)

    return {
        "statusCode": 200,
        "body": json.dumps({"generated_text":
generated_text})
    }
```
Explanation:
- **AWS Lambda**: This serverless function is triggered by an event (e.g., HTTP request) and performs inference using GPT-2.

In this chapter, we covered several deployment strategies for large language models:
1. **Exporting Models**: Use **TorchScript** and **ONNX** for model portability and deployment across different environments.
2. **Serving Models**: Use **TorchServe** for multi-model, high-performance serving, or **FastAPI** for simpler API endpoints.
3. **Cloud Deployments**: Deploy models at scale using **AWS SageMaker**, **Google AI Platform**, or **Azure ML**.
4. **Edge and Serverless Deployments**: Optimize models for deployment on **edge devices** using frameworks like **TensorFlow Lite** or **ONNX** and deploy lightweight models using **serverless platforms** like **AWS Lambda**.

By using these tools, you can deploy large language models efficiently, whether on powerful cloud infrastructures, edge devices, or serverless environments.

Code Examples
In this section, we will cover:
1. **Exporting a model to ONNX** and performing inference with it.
2. **Deploying a question-answering model** using **FastAPI** to serve the model via an API.
3. **Hands-On Project**: Deploying a **Question-Answering API** on **AWS Lambda**.

These examples will guide you step-by-step through exporting a PyTorch model to ONNX format, deploying a question-answering model with FastAPI, and running a serverless question-answering API on AWS Lambda.

---

1. Exporting a Model to ONNX and Using It for Inference

Overview of ONNX

ONNX (Open Neural Network Exchange) provides an open-source format for representing machine learning models. By converting a PyTorch model to ONNX, you can run it on other platforms like TensorFlow, Caffe2, and Microsoft's ML.NET. ONNX enables better hardware optimization and allows you to deploy models in environments that don't require PyTorch.

Steps for Exporting to ONNX:
1. **Convert the model** from PyTorch to ONNX format.
2. **Perform inference** using the ONNX model.

Code Example: Exporting PyTorch Model to ONNX

python

```python
import torch
from transformers import BertForQuestionAnswering,
BertTokenizer
import onnx
import numpy as np

# Load the pre-trained BERT model for Question
Answering
model =
BertForQuestionAnswering.from_pretrained("bert-large-
uncased-whole-word-masking-finetuned-squad")
tokenizer = BertTokenizer.from_pretrained("bert-
large-uncased-whole-word-masking-finetuned-squad")

# Set the model to evaluation mode
model.eval()

# Example input for question answering
question = "What is the capital of France?"
context = "The capital of France is Paris."
```

```python
# Tokenize the input
inputs = tokenizer(question, context,
return_tensors="pt")

# Export the model to ONNX
onnx_path = "bert_qa_model.onnx"
torch.onnx.export(model,
                    (inputs["input_ids"],
inputs["attention_mask"]),
                    onnx_path,
                    input_names=["input_ids",
"attention_mask"],
                    output_names=["start_logits",
"end_logits"],
                    dynamic_axes={"input_ids": {0:
"batch_size", 1: "sequence_length"},
                                    "attention_mask": {0:
"batch_size", 1: "sequence_length"},
                                    "start_logits": {0:
"batch_size", 1: "sequence_length"},
                                    "end_logits": {0:
"batch_size", 1: "sequence_length"}})

# Check if the model has been saved correctly
onnx_model = onnx.load(onnx_path)
onnx.checker.check_model(onnx_model)
print("ONNX model exported and verified
successfully.")
```

Explanation:
- **Exporting to ONNX**: We use torch.onnx.export() to convert the pre-trained BERT model to the ONNX format. The model expects input tokens (input_ids and attention_mask) and outputs start_logits and end_logits for the question-answering task.
- **Model Validation**: The exported ONNX model is loaded and checked using onnx.checker.check_model() to ensure it's valid.

Expected Output:

ONNX model exported and verified successfully.
Inference with ONNX:
Now, we can perform inference using the exported ONNX model. Here's how to run the inference:
python

```python
import onnxruntime as ort

# Load the ONNX model for inference
onnx_session = ort.InferenceSession(onnx_path)

# Perform inference
inputs_onnx = {
    "input_ids": inputs["input_ids"].cpu().numpy(),
    "attention_mask":
inputs["attention_mask"].cpu().numpy()
}

# Get model predictions
onnx_outputs = onnx_session.run(["start_logits",
"end_logits"], inputs_onnx)

# Convert logits to actual start and end indices
start_logits = onnx_outputs[0]
end_logits = onnx_outputs[1]

# Find the start and end token indices for the answer
start_idx = np.argmax(start_logits)
end_idx = np.argmax(end_logits)

# Convert token indices to actual answer text
answer_tokens = inputs["input_ids"][0,
start_idx:end_idx + 1]
answer = tokenizer.decode(answer_tokens)
print(f"Answer: {answer}")
```

Explanation:
- **ONNX Runtime**: onnxruntime is used to load and perform inference with the exported ONNX model.
- **Answer Extraction**: The start and end logits are used to find the span of the answer in the context. The model's output tokens are decoded to provide the final answer.

---

2. Deploying a Question-Answering Model Using FastAPI
Overview of FastAPI

FastAPI is a modern, high-performance web framework for building APIs with Python 3.7+ that is built on top of **Starlette** for the web parts and **Pydantic** for data validation. It is perfect for serving models in production environments, thanks to its speed and ease of use.

Steps to Deploy:
1. **Create a FastAPI application** that exposes the question-answering model.
2. **Define a POST endpoint** that takes a question and context, and returns the answer.
3. **Run the FastAPI app** using Uvicorn (ASGI server).

Code Example: Deploying a Question-Answering Model Using FastAPI
python

```python
from fastapi import FastAPI
from pydantic import BaseModel
from transformers import BertForQuestionAnswering,
BertTokenizer
import torch

# Initialize FastAPI app
app = FastAPI()

# Load pre-trained BERT model and tokenizer
model =
BertForQuestionAnswering.from_pretrained("bert-large-
uncased-whole-word-masking-finetuned-squad")
```

```python
tokenizer = BertTokenizer.from_pretrained("bert-
large-uncased-whole-word-masking-finetuned-squad")

class QAInput(BaseModel):
    question: str
    context: str

@app.post("/answer")
def get_answer(qa_input: QAInput):
    # Tokenize input
    inputs = tokenizer(qa_input.question,
qa_input.context, return_tensors="pt")

    # Get model predictions
    with torch.no_grad():
        start_scores, end_scores = model(**inputs)

    # Find the answer span
    start_index = torch.argmax(start_scores)
    end_index = torch.argmax(end_scores)

    # Decode the answer tokens
    answer_tokens = inputs["input_ids"][0,
start_index:end_index + 1]
    answer = tokenizer.decode(answer_tokens)

    return {"answer": answer}

# To run the app, use the following command:
# uvicorn app:app --reload
```

Explanation:
- **FastAPI**: The FastAPI app exposes a /answer POST endpoint that accepts question and context as input and returns the model's answer.
- **BERT Model**: The model uses BERT fine-tuned for the SQuAD dataset to perform question answering.

- **Tokenization**: The question and context are tokenized, passed through the model, and the answer span is extracted from the logits.

---

3. Hands-On Project: Deploy a Question-Answering API on AWS Lambda

Overview
Deploying a question-answering API on AWS Lambda is a great way to serve models without worrying about infrastructure. AWS Lambda allows you to run code in response to HTTP requests (using **API Gateway**), and you only pay for the compute time you consume.

Steps:
1. **Prepare the Model**: Fine-tune and export the model as an ONNX file.
2. **Create a Lambda Function**: Write the inference code for the Lambda function.
3. **Set up API Gateway**: Create an API that triggers the Lambda function.

Code Example: AWS Lambda Handler for Question-Answering
1. **Create the Lambda Function Handler**:

python

```python
import json
import torch
import onnxruntime as ort
from transformers import BertTokenizer

# Load the ONNX model
onnx_model_path = "gpt2_model.onnx"
onnx_session = ort.InferenceSession(onnx_model_path)
tokenizer = BertTokenizer.from_pretrained("bert-
large-uncased-whole-word-masking-finetuned-squad")

def lambda_handler(event, context):
    # Extract question and context from the event
    question =
event["queryStringParameters"]["question"]
```

```python
    context =
event["queryStringParameters"]["context"]

    # Tokenize the input
    inputs = tokenizer(question, context,
return_tensors="np")

    # Prepare inputs for ONNX model
    input_ids = inputs["input_ids"]
    attention_mask = inputs["attention_mask"]

    # Run inference with ONNX
    inputs_onnx = {
        "input_ids": input_ids,
        "attention_mask": attention_mask
    }
    start_logits, end_logits = onnx_session.run(None,
inputs_onnx)

    # Get the answer
    start_index = start_logits.argmax()
    end_index = end_logits.argmax()
    answer_tokens = input_ids[0,
start_index:end_index + 1]
    answer = tokenizer.decode(answer_tokens)

    return {
        "statusCode": 200,
        "body": json.dumps({"answer": answer})
    }
```

Explanation:
- **Lambda Handler**: The handler function processes incoming requests with a question and context, runs inference using the ONNX model, and returns the answer.
- **ONNX Runtime**: We use the onnxruntime library to load and infer from the ONNX model.
2. **Deploy the Lambda Function**:

- ○ **Create an AWS Lambda function** through the AWS Management Console or AWS CLI.
- ○ **Deploy the ONNX model** and the Lambda function code as a ZIP file or container image.
- ○ **Set up API Gateway** to trigger the Lambda function via HTTP requests.

In this chapter, we demonstrated how to:
1. **Export a PyTorch model to ONNX** for cross-platform deployment and inference.
2. **Deploy a question-answering model using FastAPI**, exposing an API endpoint for serving predictions.
3. **Deploy a serverless question-answering API on AWS Lambda**, enabling real-time inference without managing infrastructure.

These steps offer scalable solutions for deploying large language models, from edge devices to cloud services, ensuring that models can be used efficiently in production environments.

Chapter 10: Real-World Applications of LLMs

Large Language Models (LLMs) have revolutionized many industries by enabling powerful natural language processing (NLP) capabilities. From healthcare to finance, education, and more, LLMs are being utilized to solve complex problems and streamline processes. In this chapter, we will explore industry-specific use cases, how LLMs can be used to develop recommendation systems, and how to build domain-specific chatbots for enterprises.

10.1 Industry-Specific Use Cases

LLMs have vast potential to improve operational efficiency, automate workflows, and enhance decision-making across various industries. Let's explore specific use cases where LLMs have made a significant impact:

Healthcare: Clinical Trial Matching and Medical Question Answering

Clinical Trial Matching

In healthcare, LLMs can assist in matching patients with appropriate clinical trials based on their medical history, demographic data, and other relevant factors. The challenge is the large volume of clinical trial data and patient records, which makes manual matching time-consuming and prone to error.

- **Problem**: Manual analysis of clinical trial eligibility criteria and patient data is slow and resource-intensive.
- **LLM Solution**: LLMs can automate the process of reading and matching trial eligibility requirements with patient medical records, improving efficiency and increasing the number of eligible patients enrolled in trials.

Medical Question Answering

LLMs like BERT, GPT, and T5 can be trained to answer medical-related questions by understanding complex medical texts. They can provide detailed answers from clinical literature, medical textbooks, or research papers, offering quick and accurate responses for healthcare professionals.

- **Problem**: Healthcare professionals may have limited time to search for detailed medical answers.
- **LLM Solution**: LLMs can read large volumes of medical data and provide real-time, accurate answers to questions such as drug interactions, symptoms, or best treatment practices.

Example: Medical Question Answering

python

```
from transformers import pipeline

# Load a pre-trained model for question-answering
(e.g., BioBERT for medical tasks)
qa_pipeline = pipeline("question-answering",
model="dmis-lab/biobert-v1.1", tokenizer="dmis-
lab/biobert-v1.1")

context = """Clinical trials are research studies
that involve people. They are the primary method for
testing new treatments and therapies.
        Clinical trials help doctors and
researchers learn how to prevent, detect, and treat
diseases."""

question = "What are clinical trials?"

answer = qa_pipeline({"context": context, "question":
question})
print(answer['answer'])
```

Finance: Document Summarization and Fraud Detection
Document Summarization

In the finance industry, firms deal with large volumes of documents such as contracts, financial reports, and legal agreements. LLMs can automate the summarization of these documents, enabling analysts to quickly grasp the essential information without reading entire documents.

- **Problem**: Financial analysts spend significant time reviewing long documents to extract key details.
- **LLM Solution**: LLMs can generate concise summaries that highlight key financial metrics, risks, and other relevant details.

Fraud Detection

LLMs can be trained on historical transaction data to detect fraudulent activity. By analyzing patterns of behavior and identifying anomalies, LLMs can flag suspicious transactions that may require further investigation.

- **Problem**: Manual fraud detection is time-consuming and can result in delayed responses to fraudulent activities.
- **LLM Solution**: LLMs can provide real-time insights into potential fraud by analyzing transaction data and comparing it to historical patterns.

Example: Document Summarization with GPT-3

python

```python
from openai import OpenAI

openai.api_key = "your-api-key"

document = """
In 2020, the company saw a 10% decline in revenue.
This was attributed to the COVID-19 pandemic, which
significantly impacted the demand for products.
Additionally, production costs increased by 5% due to
higher material prices and supply chain disruptions.
"""

response = openai.Completion.create(
  engine="text-davinci-003",
  prompt=f"Summarize the following document:\n{document}",
  max_tokens=100
)

print(response.choices[0].text.strip())
```

Education: Personalized Learning Systems

Personalized Learning Systems

LLMs can help create personalized learning experiences by analyzing students' progress, preferences, and learning styles. By understanding how a student learns best, LLMs can tailor educational content to suit their needs.

- **Problem**: Traditional education systems often use a one-size-fits-all approach, which doesn't cater to individual learning styles.
- **LLM Solution**: LLMs can provide adaptive learning tools that recommend exercises, resources, or reading materials based on each student's performance and learning pace.

Example: Personalized Learning with an LLM

python

```
from transformers import pipeline

# Load a pre-trained model for text generation or
summarization
generator = pipeline("text-generation", model="gpt2")

student_progress = "Student has shown an
understanding of basic arithmetic but struggles with
algebra."

# Generate personalized study recommendations
recommendation = generator(f"Generate personalized
learning resources for a student with the following
progress: {student_progress}")

print(recommendation[0]['generated_text'])
```

10.2 Developing Recommendation Systems with LLMs

Overview of Recommendation Systems

Recommendation systems are essential for businesses to personalize their offerings to users. LLMs can be used to improve recommendation systems by analyzing user behavior, preferences, and textual data to recommend relevant items (e.g., movies, products, articles).

- **Collaborative Filtering**: Recommending products based on user interactions (e.g., user-item ratings).
- **Content-Based Filtering**: Recommending items based on features of the items (e.g., genre of movies, price range of products).
- **Hybrid Methods**: A combination of collaborative and content-based filtering.

Using LLMs for Recommendations

LLMs like GPT can analyze user reviews, purchase history, and product descriptions to generate personalized recommendations.

Example: Text-Based Recommendations

python

```python
from transformers import pipeline

# Load a pre-trained model for text-based
recommendations
generator = pipeline("text-generation", model="gpt2")

user_review = "I love mystery novels with complex
characters and plot twists."

# Generate recommendations based on the user's review
recommendation = generator(f"Suggest books for a user
who likes: {user_review}")

print(recommendation[0]['generated_text'])
```

10.3 Building Domain-Specific Chatbots for Enterprises

Overview

Chatbots powered by LLMs have become a key tool in enterprise environments, helping businesses automate customer service, provide real-time support, and enhance user interactions. Domain-specific chatbots are tailored to the needs of specific industries, such as healthcare, finance, or e-commerce.

Steps to Build a Domain-Specific Chatbot:
1. **Data Collection**: Collect domain-specific conversational data (e.g., customer support logs, product catalogs).
2. **Model Training or Fine-Tuning**: Fine-tune a pre-trained LLM on domain-specific data to adapt it to the required use case.
3. **Deployment**: Deploy the chatbot using web frameworks like **FastAPI** or **Flask** for API integration.

Example: Building a Domain-Specific Chatbot
Here's how you can build a domain-specific chatbot using **FastAPI** and a pre-trained LLM like GPT-3.
python

```python
from fastapi import FastAPI
from pydantic import BaseModel
import openai

openai.api_key = "your-api-key"

# Initialize FastAPI app
app = FastAPI()

class UserQuery(BaseModel):
    question: str

@app.post("/ask")
def answer_question(user_query: UserQuery):
    response = openai.Completion.create(
      engine="text-davinci-003",
      prompt=f"Answer the following customer support
question related to electronics:
{user_query.question}",
      max_tokens=150
    )
```

```
    return {"answer":
response.choices[0].text.strip()}

# Run the FastAPI app (use Uvicorn to run the app in
production)
# uvicorn app:app --reload
```

Explanation:
- **FastAPI**: We use FastAPI to expose an endpoint (/ask) where users can send questions, and the chatbot generates answers based on a pre-trained model (GPT-3 in this case).
- **OpenAI API**: The openai.Completion.create() function sends the query to the GPT-3 API and generates a relevant response.

In this chapter, we discussed real-world applications of Large Language Models (LLMs) in different industries and use cases:
1. **Healthcare**: We explored how LLMs can assist in clinical trial matching and medical question answering.
2. **Finance**: We examined how LLMs can be used for document summarization and fraud detection.
3. **Education**: We learned how LLMs can power personalized learning systems.
4. **Recommendation Systems**: We discussed how LLMs can enhance recommendation systems by analyzing textual data and user preferences.
5. **Domain-Specific Chatbots**: We saw how to build domain-specific chatbots for enterprises using FastAPI and pre-trained LLMs like GPT.

By integrating LLMs into these applications, businesses can achieve greater efficiency, personalization, and automation, ultimately enhancing customer experience and decision-making processes.

Code Examples
In this section, we will explore:
1. **Implementing a Document Summarization Pipeline** to automatically summarize documents.

2. **Training a Domain-Specific Chatbot** using fine-tuning to respond to queries related to a specific industry, such as healthcare or finance.
3. **Project**: We will create a **Custom Summarization Pipeline** specifically designed for **Legal Documents**, helping automate legal text analysis and summarization.

---

1. Implementing a Document Summarization Pipeline

Document summarization is a fundamental NLP task that condenses long documents into more digestible summaries. There are two main types of summarization:
1. **Extractive Summarization**: Selects and extracts key sentences directly from the text.
2. **Abstractive Summarization**: Generates a concise summary using new words, which may paraphrase or rephrase the original text.

In this example, we will focus on **abstractive summarization** using a pre-trained transformer model, such as **BART** or **T5**, which are specifically designed for text generation tasks like summarization.

Code Example: Using Hugging Face's transformers Library for Summarization

python

```
from transformers import pipeline

# Load the pre-trained model and tokenizer for
summarization
summarizer = pipeline("summarization",
model="facebook/bart-large-cnn")

# Sample long document
document = """
Artificial intelligence (AI) is intelligence
demonstrated by machines, in contrast to the natural
intelligence displayed by humans and animals.
Leading AI textbooks define the field as the study of
"intelligent agents": any device that perceives its
```

```
environment and takes actions that maximize its
chance of successfully achieving its goals.
As machines become increasingly capable, tasks
considered to require "intelligence" are often
removed from the definition of AI, a phenomenon known
as the AI effect.
"""

# Generate summary
summary = summarizer(document, max_length=100,
min_length=25, do_sample=False)

print("Original Document:")
print(document)
print("\nSummarized Document:")
print(summary[0]['summary_text'])
```

Explanation:
- **pipeline("summarization")**: The Hugging Face pipeline function loads a pre-trained model (here, BART for summarization) and uses it to perform summarization.
- **Document**: We provide a sample long document.
- **max_length and min_length**: These parameters control the length of the generated summary.
- **do_sample=False**: Ensures deterministic output (no randomness in the generation).

Expected Output:
vbnet

Original Document:
Artificial intelligence (AI) is intelligence demonstrated by machines, in contrast to the natural intelligence displayed by humans and animals. Leading AI textbooks define the field as the study of "intelligent agents": any device that perceives its environment and takes actions that maximize its chance of successfully achieving its goals. As machines become increasingly capable, tasks considered to require "intelligence" are often removed from the definition of AI, a phenomenon known as the AI effect.

Summarized Document:

AI is intelligence demonstrated by machines, in contrast to the natural intelligence displayed by humans and animals. AI textbooks define the field as the study of "intelligent agents": any device that perceives its environment and takes actions that maximize its chance of success.

Explanation of Results:

The summarizer successfully condensed the original text into a more compact version while maintaining the core idea. This summarization pipeline can be adapted to various types of documents, from news articles to research papers.

---

2. Training a Domain-Specific Chatbot Using Fine-Tuning

Overview of Chatbot Training

Building a domain-specific chatbot involves fine-tuning a pre-trained language model (e.g., GPT-2, BERT, T5) on domain-specific conversations. Fine-tuning involves adjusting the pre-trained model on a specific dataset to make it capable of answering questions or engaging in dialogues related to a particular field, such as healthcare, legal matters, or customer service.

In this example, we will fine-tune a pre-trained GPT-2 model to serve as a customer service chatbot for a specific domain, such as tech support.

Steps for Fine-Tuning a Domain-Specific Chatbot:

1. **Data Collection**: Gather domain-specific conversations (e.g., customer service dialogues or FAQs).
2. **Preprocess Data**: Tokenize and format the data to feed into the model.
3. **Fine-tune the Model**: Train the model on the domain-specific data.

Code Example: Fine-Tuning GPT-2 for Domain-Specific Chatbot

python

```
from transformers import GPT2LMHeadModel,
GPT2Tokenizer, Trainer, TrainingArguments
from datasets import load_dataset

# Load a pre-trained GPT-2 model and tokenizer
model = GPT2LMHeadModel.from_pretrained("gpt2")
```

```python
tokenizer = GPT2Tokenizer.from_pretrained("gpt2")

# Example domain-specific dataset (customer service
dialogues)
dataset = load_dataset("daily_dialog")

# Preprocessing: Tokenize the dialogues
def tokenize_function(examples):
    return tokenizer(examples['dialog'],
padding="max_length", truncation=True)

tokenized_dataset = dataset.map(tokenize_function,
batched=True)

# Set up training arguments
training_args = TrainingArguments(
    output_dir="./gpt2_output",
    num_train_epochs=3,
    per_device_train_batch_size=4,
    per_device_eval_batch_size=4,
    save_steps=10_000,
    logging_steps=500,
)

# Initialize Trainer
trainer = Trainer(
    model=model,
    args=training_args,
    train_dataset=tokenized_dataset["train"],
    eval_dataset=tokenized_dataset["test"]
)

# Fine-tune the model
trainer.train()

# Save the fine-tuned model
model.save_pretrained("./fine_tuned_gpt2")
```

Explanation:

- **GPT2LMHeadModel**: We load the GPT-2 model, which is a generative model suitable for dialogue generation.
- **load_dataset("daily_dialog")**: We use a domain-specific dataset of daily dialogues to fine-tune the model on conversational data.
- **tokenizer**: The tokenizer prepares the textual data into a format the model can understand.
- **TrainingArguments**: Defines the training parameters, including the number of epochs and batch size.
- **Trainer**: Hugging Face's Trainer class automates the training process.

---

3. Project: Create a Custom Summarization Pipeline for Legal Documents

Overview

Legal documents are often lengthy, complex, and difficult to interpret. A custom summarization pipeline can assist legal professionals by providing condensed versions of contracts, laws, or court rulings. We will create a summarization pipeline specifically tailored for legal documents. The steps involved are:

1. **Data Collection**: Collect a corpus of legal documents, including contracts, statutes, and court rulings.
2. **Preprocessing**: Clean and format the data for summarization.
3. **Summarization Model**: Use a pre-trained model, fine-tune it on legal text, and deploy the summarization pipeline.

Step 1: Data Collection

For this project, we will assume that you have a set of legal documents in a structured format (e.g., text or JSON). If you don't have access to a dataset, you can scrape public domain legal text from websites like **CourtListener** or use datasets from **Kaggle**.

Step 2: Preprocessing and Formatting

You can clean and prepare your legal dataset by removing irrelevant sections (such as boilerplate language) and focusing on sections that

contain important clauses or legal decisions. You might also convert PDF documents into text using a library like **PyPDF2** or **pdfminer**.
python

```python
import PyPDF2

def extract_text_from_pdf(pdf_path):
    with open(pdf_path, 'rb') as f:
        reader = PyPDF2.PdfReader(f)
        text = ""
        for page in reader.pages:
            text += page.extract_text()
    return text

# Extract text from a legal document PDF
pdf_text =
extract_text_from_pdf("legal_document.pdf")
```

Step 3: Fine-Tuning a Model for Legal Summarization
Fine-tune a summarization model, such as **BART** or **T5**, on your legal text corpus to improve its ability to generate summaries specific to legal language.
python

```python
from transformers import T5Tokenizer,
T5ForConditionalGeneration
from datasets import load_dataset

# Load pre-trained T5 model and tokenizer
model =
T5ForConditionalGeneration.from_pretrained("t5-base")
tokenizer = T5Tokenizer.from_pretrained("t5-base")

# Load your legal documents dataset
dataset = load_dataset("path/to/legal_data")

# Tokenize the dataset
def tokenize_function(examples):
    return tokenizer(examples['text'],
padding="max_length", truncation=True)
```

```python
tokenized_data = dataset.map(tokenize_function,
batched=True)

# Fine-tune T5 model on legal data
from transformers import Trainer, TrainingArguments

training_args = TrainingArguments(
    output_dir="./legal_summary_model",
    num_train_epochs=3,
    per_device_train_batch_size=4,
    logging_steps=500,
)

trainer = Trainer(
    model=model,
    args=training_args,
    train_dataset=tokenized_data["train"],
    eval_dataset=tokenized_data["test"]
)

trainer.train()
model.save_pretrained("./legal_summary_model")
```

Explanation:
- **T5 for Summarization**: T5 is fine-tuned on a legal dataset to improve its summarization capabilities, focusing on condensing legal documents into key points.
- **Data Preprocessing**: Text is tokenized to fit the model input requirements. We focus on sections of the document that are most relevant to legal professionals.

Step 4: Deploy the Summarization Pipeline
Once the model is fine-tuned, you can deploy it as a web service using **FastAPI** or any other web framework. Here's an example using **FastAPI**:
python

```python
from fastapi import FastAPI
from pydantic import BaseModel
```

```python
from transformers import T5ForConditionalGeneration,
T5Tokenizer

app = FastAPI()

# Load the fine-tuned model and tokenizer
model =
T5ForConditionalGeneration.from_pretrained("./legal_s
ummary_model")
tokenizer =
T5Tokenizer.from_pretrained("./legal_summary_model")

class LegalDocument(BaseModel):
    document_text: str

@app.post("/summarize")
def summarize_document(doc: LegalDocument):
    inputs = tokenizer(doc.document_text,
return_tensors="pt", padding=True, truncation=True)
    summary_ids = model.generate(inputs["input_ids"],
max_length=150, min_length=50, length_penalty=2.0)
    summary = tokenizer.decode(summary_ids[0],
skip_special_tokens=True)
    return {"summary": summary}

# To run the FastAPI app (use Uvicorn for production)
# uvicorn app:app --reload
```

Explanation:

- **FastAPI**: This API accepts a POST request with the legal document text, processes it using the fine-tuned model, and returns the summary.
- **Model Deployment**: You can deploy the API on a cloud platform like AWS, GCP, or Azure, or run it locally for quick testing.

In this chapter, we:

1. Implemented a **document summarization pipeline** using pre-trained models like BART or T5, tailored for condensing long documents into concise summaries.

2. Trained a **domain-specific chatbot** by fine-tuning a pre-trained GPT-2 model on a customer service dataset, making the chatbot capable of answering industry-specific queries.
3. Built a **custom summarization pipeline for legal documents**, using a legal dataset to fine-tune a T5 model and deploy it through FastAPI for real-time summarization.

These techniques can be applied to a wide variety of domains, allowing businesses and professionals to automate and optimize the processing of complex documents, improving efficiency and decision-making in real-world applications.

Chapter 11: Scaling and Distributed Training

As models grow in size and complexity, training them on a single machine becomes increasingly impractical due to memory and computational limitations. Distributed training enables models to be trained across multiple GPUs or even multiple nodes in a cluster. In this chapter, we will explore several methods to scale and distribute model training efficiently, using tools like **Distributed Data Parallel (DDP)** in PyTorch, **Fully Sharded Data Parallel (FSDP)**, and **DeepSpeed**. We will also discuss training workflows on cloud platforms like **Google Colab**, **AWS SageMaker**, and **Azure ML**.

11.1 Scaling Models with Distributed Data Parallel (DDP) in PyTorch

What is Distributed Data Parallel (DDP)?
Distributed Data Parallel (DDP) is a PyTorch feature that allows you to scale training by parallelizing across multiple GPUs. DDP works by replicating the model across multiple devices (GPUs) and splitting the data into mini-batches. Each GPU computes gradients on a mini-batch, and after each backward pass, DDP synchronizes the gradients across all GPUs to ensure that each model replica learns in parallel. This significantly speeds up training by reducing the time needed to process large datasets.

Key Benefits of DDP:
1. **Faster Training**: By distributing the work across multiple GPUs, training time is reduced.
2. **Memory Efficiency**: Each GPU handles only a portion of the data, reducing the memory footprint required for large models.
3. **Scalability**: DDP can scale to many GPUs on a single machine or across multiple machines, providing flexibility for large-scale training.

Code Example: Setting Up DDP for Multi-GPU Training

To implement DDP, we need to follow these steps:

1. Initialize the process group.
2. Wrap the model in DistributedDataParallel.
3. Ensure each GPU processes a unique subset of the dataset.

python

```python
import torch
import torch.nn as nn
import torch.optim as optim
import torch.distributed as dist
from torch.nn.parallel import DistributedDataParallel
as DDP
from torch.utils.data import DataLoader,
DistributedSampler
from torchvision import datasets, transforms
import os

# Initialize the process group for distributed
training
dist.init_process_group(backend="nccl")

# Define a simple neural network model
class SimpleModel(nn.Module):
    def __init__(self):
        super(SimpleModel, self).__init__()
        self.fc1 = nn.Linear(784, 128)
        self.fc2 = nn.Linear(128, 10)

    def forward(self, x):
        x = torch.relu(self.fc1(x))
        x = self.fc2(x)
        return x

# Initialize the model and move it to GPU
model = SimpleModel().to(torch.device("cuda"))
model = DDP(model,
device_ids=[torch.cuda.current_device()])
```

```python
# Define a dataset and data loader
transform =
transforms.Compose([transforms.ToTensor(),
transforms.Normalize((0.5,), (0.5,))])
dataset = datasets.MNIST(root='./data', train=True,
download=True, transform=transform)
sampler = DistributedSampler(dataset)
data_loader = DataLoader(dataset, batch_size=64,
sampler=sampler)

# Define optimizer
optimizer = optim.SGD(model.parameters(), lr=0.01)

# Training loop
for epoch in range(5):
    model.train()
    sampler.set_epoch(epoch)   # Ensure different
shuffle order on each epoch
    for inputs, targets in data_loader:
        inputs, targets = inputs.view(-1,
28*28).to(torch.device("cuda")),
targets.to(torch.device("cuda"))

        optimizer.zero_grad()
        outputs = model(inputs)
        loss = nn.CrossEntropyLoss()(outputs,
targets)

        loss.backward()
        optimizer.step()

    print(f"Epoch {epoch+1}, Loss: {loss.item()}")

# Cleanup the distributed training process group
dist.destroy_process_group()
```

Explanation:
- **dist.init_process_group()**: Initializes the distributed training environment.
- **DistributedDataParallel**: This wrapper ensures that each GPU performs its own forward and backward pass and then synchronizes the gradients across all devices.
- **Data Loader with DistributedSampler**: This ensures that the data is distributed properly across the GPUs, so each GPU gets a different subset of the dataset.

11.2 Fully Sharded Data Parallel (FSDP) and DeepSpeed for Large Models

What is Fully Sharded Data Parallel (FSDP)?
FSDP is an advanced technique in PyTorch for training very large models. Unlike DDP, which replicates the entire model across GPUs, FSDP shards the model into smaller chunks and distributes them across the GPUs. This allows for better memory usage and the ability to train models that would otherwise not fit into the memory of a single GPU.

Key Benefits of FSDP:
1. **Efficient Memory Usage**: By sharding the model, memory usage is significantly reduced, enabling the training of larger models.
2. **Scalability**: FSDP allows for the scaling of models across many GPUs with reduced memory overhead per GPU.

What is DeepSpeed?
DeepSpeed is a deep learning optimization library developed by Microsoft that is designed to enable efficient training of massive models. It integrates well with PyTorch and provides several features, including:
- **Zero Redundancy Optimizer (ZeRO)**: This optimizes memory and computation by reducing redundant operations during training.
- **Model Parallelism**: DeepSpeed provides support for training models that don't fit into a single GPU's memory by splitting the model across multiple GPUs.

Code Example: Using DeepSpeed for Efficient Training
python

```python
import deepspeed
from transformers import GPT2LMHeadModel,
GPT2Tokenizer

# Load a pre-trained GPT-2 model and tokenizer
model = GPT2LMHeadModel.from_pretrained("gpt2")
tokenizer = GPT2Tokenizer.from_pretrained("gpt2")

# Define the training parameters
deepspeed_config = {
    "train_batch_size": 4,
    "gradient_accumulation_steps": 8,
    "zero_optimization": {
        "stage": 2,   # ZeRO stage 2 optimizes memory
        "offload_optimizer": {"device": "cpu"},
        "offload_param": {"device": "cpu"}
    }
}

# Initialize the model with DeepSpeed
model_engine, optimizer, _, _ =
deepspeed.initialize(config=deepspeed_config,
model=model)

# Prepare a dataset and data loader
inputs = tokenizer("DeepSpeed allows for efficient
training of large models", return_tensors="pt")
inputs = inputs.to(model.device)

# Forward pass with DeepSpeed
outputs = model_engine(**inputs)

# Loss calculation and backward pass
loss = outputs.loss
model_engine.backward(loss)
model_engine.step()
```

Explanation:
- **DeepSpeed Initialization**: We initialize DeepSpeed with a configuration that optimizes memory usage using ZeRO optimization.
- **Training with DeepSpeed**: The model is trained using DeepSpeed's memory-efficient training pipeline, allowing for the training of large models.

11.3 Training Multi-Billion-Parameter Models Across GPUs and Nodes

Overview

Training models with billions of parameters requires specialized techniques and infrastructure. To train such massive models, you need to distribute both the data and the model across multiple GPUs and nodes. Techniques like **data parallelism**, **model parallelism**, and **pipeline parallelism** help distribute the work.
- **Data Parallelism**: The model is replicated across all GPUs, and each GPU processes a subset of the data.
- **Model Parallelism**: The model is split across multiple GPUs, with each GPU handling a different part of the model.
- **Pipeline Parallelism**: The model is split into stages, with each GPU or node processing a different stage.

Key Strategies for Training Large Models:
1. **Multi-GPU Setup**: Use multiple GPUs to split the data and parallelize training.
2. **Model Parallelism**: Divide the model's layers and run them on different GPUs.
3. **Pipeline Parallelism**: Split the forward and backward passes into stages and distribute them across different devices.

11.4 Cloud-Based Training Workflows

Overview of Cloud-Based Training

Cloud platforms provide scalable resources for training large models without the need for on-premises infrastructure. Services like **Google Colab**, **AWS SageMaker**, and **Azure ML** allow you to leverage powerful GPUs and TPUs to train models efficiently.

Google Colab:
- **Free Access**: Colab provides free access to GPUs and TPUs, making it ideal for smaller-scale experiments.
- **Easy Setup**: Colab offers an easy-to-use Jupyter notebook interface for quick experimentation.
- **Limitations**: While Colab is free, it has resource limitations like limited GPU usage time per session.

AWS SageMaker:
- **Fully Managed Service**: SageMaker provides an end-to-end managed service for training, tuning, and deploying machine learning models.
- **Scalability**: With support for large-scale training using distributed infrastructure, SageMaker allows you to easily scale to multiple GPUs or even across multiple nodes.
- **Integration with AWS**: SageMaker integrates seamlessly with other AWS services, including data storage and monitoring.

Azure ML:
- **Enterprise-Level Tools**: Azure ML provides robust tools for building, training, and deploying machine learning models at scale.
- **Multi-Node Scaling**: Azure ML can scale training across multiple GPUs and nodes, allowing you to train very large models.
- **Integration with Azure Services**: Azure ML integrates with other Azure services for data storage, compute, and monitoring.

Code Example: Using SageMaker for Distributed Training

python

```python
import sagemaker
from sagemaker import get_execution_role
from sagemaker.pytorch import PyTorchModel

# Define the role and model
role = get_execution_role()
model = PyTorchModel(model_data="s3://path-to-
model/model.tar.gz", role=role)

# Define the training job configuration
estimator = model.fit(inputs={"training": "s3://path-
to-training-data/"})

# Deploy the model
predictor =
model.deploy(instance_type="ml.p3.2xlarge",
initial_instance_count=1)

# Make predictions
result = predictor.predict(data)
print(result)
```

Explanation:
- **SageMaker Model**: We load the pre-trained model stored in an S3 bucket.
- **Distributed Training**: The fit() method launches a distributed training job using SageMaker's resources.
- **Deployment**: After training, the model is deployed for real-time inference on a powerful GPU instance.

In this chapter, we:
1. Explored **Distributed Data Parallel (DDP)** for scaling models across multiple GPUs to accelerate training.
2. Delved into **Fully Sharded Data Parallel (FSDP)** and **DeepSpeed** to efficiently train large models with reduced memory overhead.

3. Discussed **multi-billion-parameter model training** strategies, including data parallelism, model parallelism, and pipeline parallelism for distributed training across GPUs and nodes.
4. Walked through cloud-based training solutions like **Google Colab**, **AWS SageMaker**, and **Azure ML**, providing a scalable and flexible approach to model training.

These techniques and tools are crucial for scaling the training of large models in the real world, enabling researchers and enterprises to handle the growing complexity and size of modern deep learning models.

Code Examples

In this section, we will explore:
1. **Training a Model with PyTorch Distributed Data Parallel (DDP)**.
2. **Scaling a Transformer Model with DeepSpeed**.
3. **Hands-On Project**: Training a Multi-GPU Transformer Model using DeepSpeed.

These examples will guide you through setting up distributed training using PyTorch's **DDP**, scaling a Transformer model with **DeepSpeed**, and utilizing **multi-GPU** setups for efficient model training.

---

1. Training a Model with PyTorch Distributed Data Parallel (DDP)
Overview of PyTorch DDP
Distributed Data Parallel (DDP) is a PyTorch feature that enables the parallelization of training across multiple GPUs. It works by replicating the model across multiple devices and splitting the dataset into mini-batches. Each GPU computes gradients on a mini-batch of data, and the gradients are synchronized across all GPUs after the backward pass. This allows for faster training by leveraging multiple GPUs in parallel.

Key Concepts:
- **Initialization**: The distributed environment must be initialized before using DDP.
- **Data Parallelism**: Each GPU computes gradients on a subset of the data and synchronizes gradients after each backward pass.
- **Gradient Synchronization**: The gradients are averaged across GPUs after each backward pass.

Code Example: PyTorch DDP Setup for Multi-GPU Training
python

```python
import torch
import torch.nn as nn
import torch.optim as optim
import torch.distributed as dist
from torch.nn.parallel import DistributedDataParallel
as DDP
from torch.utils.data import DataLoader,
DistributedSampler
from torchvision import datasets, transforms
import os

# Initialize the distributed environment
dist.init_process_group(backend="nccl")

# Define the model
class SimpleModel(nn.Module):
    def __init__(self):
        super(SimpleModel, self).__init__()
        self.fc1 = nn.Linear(784, 128)
        self.fc2 = nn.Linear(128, 10)

    def forward(self, x):
        x = torch.relu(self.fc1(x))
        x = self.fc2(x)
        return x

# Initialize the model and move it to the current
device (GPU)
device = torch.device("cuda")
model = SimpleModel().to(device)
model = DDP(model,
device_ids=[torch.cuda.current_device()])

# Define a dataset and DataLoader
```

```python
transform =
transforms.Compose([transforms.ToTensor(),
transforms.Normalize((0.5,), (0.5,))])
dataset = datasets.MNIST(root='./data', train=True,
download=True, transform=transform)
sampler = DistributedSampler(dataset)
data_loader = DataLoader(dataset, batch_size=64,
sampler=sampler)

# Define the optimizer
optimizer = optim.SGD(model.parameters(), lr=0.01)

# Training loop
for epoch in range(5):
    model.train()
    sampler.set_epoch(epoch)   # Ensures different
shuffle order on each epoch
    for inputs, targets in data_loader:
        inputs, targets = inputs.view(-1,
28*28).to(device), targets.to(device)

        optimizer.zero_grad()
        outputs = model(inputs)
        loss = nn.CrossEntropyLoss()(outputs,
targets)

        loss.backward()
        optimizer.step()

    print(f"Epoch {epoch+1}, Loss: {loss.item()}")

# Cleanup the distributed environment
dist.destroy_process_group()
```

Explanation:
1. **dist.init_process_group()**: Initializes the distributed environment, allowing communication between GPUs.
2. **DistributedDataParallel**: Wraps the model with DDP to enable data parallelism. The model is replicated across multiple GPUs.

3. **DistributedSampler**: Ensures that each GPU processes a unique subset of the data.
4. **Training Loop**: During each epoch, gradients are calculated on different GPUs, and they are synchronized and averaged after the backward pass.
5. **dist.destroy_process_group()**: Cleans up the distributed environment after training is finished.

Expected Output:

python

Epoch 1, Loss: 0.1985
Epoch 2, Loss: 0.1601

...

---

2. Scaling a Transformer Model with DeepSpeed

Overview of DeepSpeed

DeepSpeed is a deep learning optimization library developed by Microsoft that is designed to enable the efficient training of massive models. It integrates seamlessly with PyTorch and offers several features to optimize training, including:

- **Zero Redundancy Optimizer (ZeRO)**: Efficiently reduces memory usage and computation by eliminating redundant operations during training.
- **Model Parallelism**: Allows splitting a model across multiple GPUs to handle larger models that do not fit into a single GPU's memory.
- **Mixed Precision Training**: Automatically uses mixed precision (FP16) to reduce memory usage and speed up training.

Key Features:
1. **ZeRO Optimization**: Reduces memory usage by partitioning gradients, optimizer states, and model parameters.
2. **Memory Efficiency**: DeepSpeed is particularly effective when training large models with billions of parameters.
3. **Model Parallelism**: Enables training of models that don't fit in the memory of a single GPU by splitting the model across multiple GPUs.

Code Example: Scaling a Transformer Model with DeepSpeed
python

```python
import deepspeed
from transformers import GPT2LMHeadModel,
GPT2Tokenizer
from torch.utils.data import DataLoader
from datasets import load_dataset

# Load pre-trained GPT-2 model and tokenizer
model = GPT2LMHeadModel.from_pretrained("gpt2")
tokenizer = GPT2Tokenizer.from_pretrained("gpt2")

# Load a dataset (e.g., text generation dataset)
dataset = load_dataset("wikitext", "wikitext-103-raw-
v1")
train_data = dataset["train"]

# Tokenize the dataset
def tokenize_function(examples):
    return tokenizer(examples['text'],
padding="max_length", truncation=True)

train_data = train_data.map(tokenize_function,
batched=True)

# Define training parameters
deepspeed_config = {
    "train_batch_size": 4,
    "gradient_accumulation_steps": 8,
    "zero_optimization": {
        "stage": 2,   # ZeRO stage 2 optimizes memory
        "offload_optimizer": {"device": "cpu"},
        "offload_param": {"device": "cpu"}
    }
}

# Initialize DeepSpeed engine
```

```
model_engine, optimizer, _, _ =
deepspeed.initialize(config=deepspeed_config,
model=model)

# Define DataLoader
train_dataloader = DataLoader(train_data,
batch_size=4)

# Training loop with DeepSpeed
for epoch in range(3):
    model_engine.train()
    for step, batch in enumerate(train_dataloader):
        inputs = tokenizer(batch["text"],
return_tensors="pt", padding=True, truncation=True)
        inputs = inputs.to(model.device)

        # Forward pass
        outputs = model_engine(**inputs)
        loss = outputs.loss

        # Backward pass
        model_engine.backward(loss)
        model_engine.step()

    print(f"Epoch {epoch+1}, Loss: {loss.item()}")
```

Explanation:

- **DeepSpeed Configuration**: The DeepSpeed configuration specifies how to optimize memory usage using ZeRO (Stage 2), offloading model parameters and optimizer states to CPU memory.
- **Data Loading**: The dataset is tokenized using the GPT-2 tokenizer, and we use DeepSpeed's memory-efficient setup to train the model.
- **deepspeed.initialize()**: Initializes the DeepSpeed engine with the model and configuration, enabling distributed and memory-efficient training.

3. Hands-On: Train a Multi-GPU Transformer Model Using DeepSpeed

Overview

In this hands-on project, we will use DeepSpeed to train a **Transformer-based model** (like **GPT-2**) on **multiple GPUs**. This will involve setting up a multi-GPU environment using **DeepSpeed's ZeRO optimization** to efficiently distribute the model and data across multiple devices. By using DeepSpeed, we can scale the model training and fit larger models that wouldn't fit in the memory of a single GPU.

Steps to Train the Model:
1. **Prepare the Dataset**: Load and preprocess the dataset for training.
2. **Configure DeepSpeed**: Set up DeepSpeed for multi-GPU training with ZeRO optimization.
3. **Train the Model**: Fine-tune the Transformer model on the dataset using multiple GPUs.

Code Example: Multi-GPU Training with DeepSpeed
python

```python
import deepspeed
from transformers import GPT2LMHeadModel,
GPT2Tokenizer
from torch.utils.data import DataLoader
from datasets import load_dataset
import torch

# Load the GPT-2 model and tokenizer
model = GPT2LMHeadModel.from_pretrained("gpt2")
tokenizer = GPT2Tokenizer.from_pretrained("gpt2")

# Load dataset (e.g., Wikitext dataset)
dataset = load_dataset("wikitext", "wikitext-103-raw-
v1")
train_data = dataset["train"]

# Tokenize dataset
def tokenize_function(examples):
```

```python
    return tokenizer(examples['text'],
padding="max_length", truncation=True)

train_data = train_data.map(tokenize_function,
batched=True)

# Define DeepSpeed configuration
deepspeed_config = {
    "train_batch_size": 8,
    "gradient_accumulation_steps": 16,
    "zero_optimization": {
        "stage": 3,  # ZeRO stage 3 splits the
optimizer, model parameters, and gradients
        "offload_optimizer": {"device": "cpu"},
        "offload_param": {"device": "cpu"}
    }
}

# Initialize the model with DeepSpeed
model_engine, optimizer, _, _ =
deepspeed.initialize(config=deepspeed_config,
model=model)

# Create DataLoader for training
train_dataloader = DataLoader(train_data,
batch_size=8)

# Multi-GPU Training Loop with DeepSpeed
for epoch in range(5):
    model_engine.train()
    for step, batch in enumerate(train_dataloader):
        inputs = tokenizer(batch["text"],
return_tensors="pt", padding=True, truncation=True)
        inputs = inputs.to(model.device)

        # Forward pass
        outputs = model_engine(**inputs)
        loss = outputs.loss
```

```
# Backward pass
model_engine.backward(loss)
model_engine.step()

print(f"Epoch {epoch+1}, Loss: {loss.item()}")
```
Explanation:
- **ZeRO Stage 3**: In ZeRO stage 3, DeepSpeed optimizes memory by partitioning not just the model parameters but also the optimizer states and gradients across multiple GPUs. This allows training larger models with even fewer resources.
- **Multi-GPU Setup**: By leveraging DeepSpeed's multi-GPU and memory optimization features, we can scale our model training across multiple GPUs, improving training speed and enabling the training of larger models.

In this chapter, we covered several advanced techniques for scaling and distributed training:
1. **Distributed Data Parallel (DDP)**: We demonstrated how to use PyTorch's DDP for multi-GPU training, where the model is replicated across devices, and each device handles a subset of the data.
2. **DeepSpeed**: We explored how to scale Transformer models using DeepSpeed, including its **ZeRO optimization** for efficient memory usage, enabling the training of large models even with limited resources.
3. **Hands-On Training**: We provided a comprehensive hands-on example of training a multi-GPU Transformer model using DeepSpeed, demonstrating how to scale the training process to handle larger datasets and more complex models.

These techniques will help you efficiently scale the training of large models, making it feasible to train multi-billion-parameter models using distributed infrastructure.

Chapter 12: Interpretability and Debugging

As models become increasingly complex, understanding their decision-making process becomes more challenging but essential. **Interpretability** and **debugging** are crucial aspects of ensuring that deep learning models, including Large Language Models (LLMs), are functioning as expected and can be trusted in real-world applications. This chapter will explore methods for visualizing model behavior, debugging common issues in training LLMs, and utilizing tools like **Captum** for explainable AI.

12.1 Visualizing Attention Maps for Model Predictions

Overview of Attention Mechanisms in LLMs
Attention mechanisms, particularly **self-attention**, are central to the performance of transformer-based models like **BERT**, **GPT**, and **T5**. The attention mechanism allows the model to weigh the importance of different words in a sequence when making predictions, enabling it to capture long-range dependencies effectively.

Visualizing attention maps can provide insights into how the model is making decisions. By examining which words or tokens the model attends to most during its predictions, we can gain a better understanding of its behavior and identify potential issues such as bias or overfitting.

What Are Attention Maps?
Attention maps represent the attention scores for each token pair (i.e., how much attention a given token pays to another token) in a sequence. These maps can be visualized as matrices where the x-axis represents the tokens in the input, and the y-axis represents the tokens in the output. Each value in the matrix represents the attention score between the two tokens.

Visualizing Attention with PyTorch and Hugging Face Transformers
To visualize attention maps in a transformer model, we need to extract
the attention weights during the model's forward pass and then plot
them.

Code Example: Visualizing Attention Maps
python

```python
import torch
import matplotlib.pyplot as plt
from transformers import BertTokenizer,
BertForSequenceClassification
import seaborn as sns

# Load pre-trained BERT model and tokenizer
model =
BertForSequenceClassification.from_pretrained("bert-
base-uncased", output_attentions=True)
tokenizer = BertTokenizer.from_pretrained("bert-base-
uncased")

# Define input text
text = "The quick brown fox jumps over the lazy dog."

# Tokenize input text
inputs = tokenizer(text, return_tensors="pt")

# Forward pass with attention outputs
outputs = model(**inputs)
attentions = outputs.attentions  # List of attention
scores from all layers

# Select the attention map of the last layer (for
simplicity)
attention_map = attentions[-1]  # Attention from the
last layer

# Get the attention weights for the first head (layer
12, head 0)
```

```
attention_weights =
attention_map[0][0].detach().numpy()

# Plot the attention map
sns.heatmap(attention_weights,
xticklabels=inputs.tokens(),
yticklabels=inputs.tokens(), cmap="Blues")
plt.title("Attention Map for 'The quick brown fox
jumps over the lazy dog.'")
plt.show()
```

Explanation:

1. **output_attentions=True**: We specify this parameter when loading the pre-trained model so that the model returns attention weights during the forward pass.
2. **Extract Attention Weights**: The attentions variable contains a list of attention maps, with each element corresponding to a layer's attention scores. We select the last layer for visualization.
3. **Plotting**: Using **Seaborn's heatmap**, we plot the attention weights for the first attention head in the last layer. The x and y labels represent the tokens in the input text.

Expected Output:

A heatmap showing how the model attends to different tokens in the input sequence during its prediction. Darker regions in the heatmap indicate higher attention.

12.2 Debugging Common Training Issues in LLMs

Training Large Language Models (LLMs) can be challenging, especially with large datasets and models. Debugging training issues in LLMs is essential for ensuring that models converge effectively and avoid overfitting or underfitting.

Common Issues in LLM Training

1. **Vanishing or Exploding Gradients**:

- o **Cause**: During backpropagation, gradients can either become too small (vanishing gradients) or too large (exploding gradients), making training unstable.
- o **Solution**: Use gradient clipping or initialize weights properly to avoid extreme values.

2. **Overfitting**:
- o **Cause**: The model memorizes the training data, leading to poor generalization on the test data.
- o **Solution**: Use techniques like dropout, early stopping, and regularization to prevent overfitting.

3. **Slow Convergence**:
- o **Cause**: The model might not be learning quickly enough, possibly due to a poor learning rate or insufficient data.
- o **Solution**: Adjust the learning rate or use a learning rate scheduler to improve convergence speed.

4. **Training Instability (NaN Loss)**:
- o **Cause**: NaN (Not a Number) loss values can arise due to improper initialization, high learning rates, or numerical instability.
- o **Solution**: Monitor gradients and loss values during training, and consider using mixed precision training to stabilize training.

Debugging Strategy:
1. **Monitor Gradients**:
- o You can track the magnitude of gradients during training to identify vanishing or exploding gradients. If the gradients are excessively large or small, consider using gradient clipping or adjusting the learning rate.

python

```
# Monitor gradients
for param in model.parameters():
    if param.grad is not None:
        print(f"Max Gradient for {param.name}:
{param.grad.max()}")
```

2. **Use Learning Rate Schedulers**:
- o Learning rate schedulers, like **ReduceLROnPlateau** or **CosineAnnealingLR**, can help adjust the learning rate dynamically during training, ensuring faster convergence.

python

```python
from torch.optim.lr_scheduler import
ReduceLROnPlateau

scheduler = ReduceLROnPlateau(optimizer, 'min',
patience=5)
```

3. **Check Loss Values**:
   o Constantly monitor the loss value to detect issues like NaNs, and adjust your learning rate or optimizer settings accordingly.

python

```python
if torch.isnan(loss):
    print("NaN detected in loss, terminating
training")
    break
```

12.3 Tools for Explainable AI

Overview of Explainable AI (XAI)
Explainable AI (XAI) is an area of AI that focuses on making machine learning models more transparent and interpretable. For LLMs, this can mean understanding how they make predictions, especially for tasks like classification or text generation.

Captum: A Library for Model Interpretability
Captum is an open-source library developed by Facebook that provides tools for model interpretability and understanding. It allows users to visualize and interpret how neural networks make decisions. Captum supports several attribution methods, including:
- **Integrated Gradients**: Measures the contribution of each feature to the model's prediction.
- **Layer-wise Relevance Propagation (LRP)**: Highlights the most relevant features for the model's decision.
- **GradientSHAP**: Combines SHAP values with gradients to provide insight into model behavior.

Using Captum to Interpret Model Predictions
python

```python
import torch
from captum.attr import IntegratedGradients
from transformers import BertTokenizer,
BertForSequenceClassification

# Load model and tokenizer
model =
BertForSequenceClassification.from_pretrained("bert-
base-uncased")
tokenizer = BertTokenizer.from_pretrained("bert-base-
uncased")

# Tokenize input text
text = "This is a great movie!"
inputs = tokenizer(text, return_tensors="pt",
padding=True, truncation=True)

# Define Integrated Gradients for attribution
ig = IntegratedGradients(model)

# Get model predictions
inputs = inputs.to(model.device)
predictions = model(**inputs).logits
target = torch.argmax(predictions)

# Compute attributions
attributions, delta =
ig.attribute(inputs['input_ids'], target=target,
return_convergence_delta=True)

# Visualize the attributions
import matplotlib.pyplot as plt
attributions = attributions.sum(dim=-
1).squeeze().cpu().detach().numpy()
```

```
tokens =
tokenizer.convert_ids_to_tokens(inputs['input_ids'].s
queeze().cpu().numpy())
plt.bar(tokens, attributions)
plt.xticks(rotation=90)
plt.title("Attribution Scores for Each Token in the
Sentence")
plt.show()
```

Explanation:
1. **Captum**: We use Captum's IntegratedGradients to compute attributions, which indicate how much each token contributes to the model's prediction.
2. **Visualization**: The attribution scores are visualized using a bar plot where the height of each bar represents the contribution of each token to the prediction.

Expected Output:
A bar plot that displays the contribution of each token in the sentence "This is a great movie!" to the model's classification.

In this chapter, we explored the importance of **interpretability** and **debugging** in Large Language Models (LLMs):
1. **Visualizing Attention Maps**: We learned how to visualize attention maps, which help understand which parts of the input sequence the model focuses on during predictions.
2. **Debugging Training Issues**: Common training issues like vanishing gradients, overfitting, slow convergence, and NaN loss were discussed, along with strategies for addressing them.
3. **Tools for Explainable AI**: We introduced **Captum**, an open-source library for model interpretability, and demonstrated how to use it for attribution tasks, specifically using **Integrated Gradients** to understand model decisions.

By incorporating these techniques into your workflow, you can enhance your understanding of model behavior, improve training stability, and make more informed decisions when deploying models in real-world applications.

Code Examples

In this section, we will cover:

1. **Using Captum to Visualize Feature Importance in Model Predictions**: We will demonstrate how to use Captum, an interpretability library, to understand how the features (tokens or words) in an input influence the predictions made by a transformer model.

2. **Debugging a Transformer Model's Training Loop**: We will walk through strategies and methods for debugging common issues in a Transformer model's training loop, including dealing with vanishing gradients, loss spikes, and slow convergence.

---

1. Using Captum to Visualize Feature Importance in Model Predictions

Overview of Captum

Captum is a powerful interpretability tool developed by Facebook for PyTorch. It helps explain and visualize how different features of the input (such as words or tokens in text data) contribute to the model's predictions. It provides several methods for attribution, including **Integrated Gradients**, **Layer-wise Relevance Propagation (LRP)**, and **GradientSHAP**.

In this example, we will use **Integrated Gradients** to explain the feature importance in the predictions of a **BERT model**. Integrated Gradients helps to compute how much each input feature contributes to a given prediction by comparing the model's output when the input is at its baseline (e.g., a tensor of zeros) versus its actual value.

Code Example: Using Captum to Visualize Feature Importance
python

```python
import torch
import matplotlib.pyplot as plt
from captum.attr import IntegratedGradients
from transformers import BertTokenizer,
BertForSequenceClassification

# Load the pre-trained BERT model and tokenizer
```

```python
model =
BertForSequenceClassification.from_pretrained("bert-
base-uncased")
tokenizer = BertTokenizer.from_pretrained("bert-base-
uncased")

# Example input text for feature importance
visualization
text = "Deep learning models are great for solving
complex problems."

# Tokenize the input text
inputs = tokenizer(text, return_tensors="pt",
padding=True, truncation=True)

# Move the model and inputs to the device (GPU or
CPU)
device = torch.device("cuda" if
torch.cuda.is_available() else "cpu")
model.to(device)
inputs = {key: value.to(device) for key, value in
inputs.items()}

# Define Integrated Gradients for feature attribution
ig = IntegratedGradients(model)

# Get model predictions
model.eval()
predictions = model(**inputs).logits
target_class = torch.argmax(predictions)

# Compute the attributions (feature importance)
attributions, delta =
ig.attribute(inputs['input_ids'],
target=target_class, return_convergence_delta=True)

# Visualize the attributions
attributions_sum = attributions.sum(dim=-
1).squeeze().cpu().detach().numpy()
```

```
# Convert token IDs to actual tokens for better
visualization
tokens =
tokenizer.convert_ids_to_tokens(inputs['input_ids'].s
queeze().cpu().numpy())

# Plot the feature importance for each token
plt.figure(figsize=(10, 5))
plt.bar(tokens, attributions_sum)
plt.xticks(rotation=90)
plt.title(f"Feature Importance for the Sentence:
'{text}'")
plt.xlabel("Tokens")
plt.ylabel("Attribution Score")
plt.show()
```

Explanation:
1. **IntegratedGradients**: We use Captum's **Integrated Gradients** method, which compares the model's output with the baseline (zero input) and computes the importance of each feature.
2. **Tokenization**: We tokenize the input sentence using the BERT tokenizer, and the tokens are then fed into the BERT model.
3. **Attribution Calculation**: We use the .attribute() method to compute the attributions for each token. This gives us the feature importance for each token in the input sentence.
4. **Visualization**: The importance of each token is plotted in a bar chart, where the height of each bar represents the degree to which the token contributes to the model's prediction.

Expected Output:
A bar plot that displays the contribution of each token in the sentence to the model's prediction. Tokens with higher bars indicate features that have more influence on the model's decision.

---

2. Debugging a Transformer Model's Training Loop

Overview of Common Training Issues

Training Transformer models can be challenging due to their complexity and the large number of parameters. Common issues during training include:

1. **Vanishing and Exploding Gradients**: These issues can cause the model to either not learn effectively (vanishing gradients) or become unstable (exploding gradients).
2. **Loss Spikes or NaNs**: Training can sometimes result in spikes in loss or NaN values, often caused by numerical instability.
3. **Slow Convergence**: The model might be training very slowly, possibly due to a high learning rate or insufficient data.

To debug these issues, we will implement strategies such as:

- **Gradient Clipping** to prevent exploding gradients.
- **Monitoring Gradients** to identify vanishing or exploding gradients.
- **Loss Monitoring** to detect NaNs or spikes.

Code Example: Debugging a Transformer Model's Training Loop
python

```python
import torch
from transformers import
BertForSequenceClassification, BertTokenizer
from torch.optim import AdamW

# Initialize model and tokenizer
model =
BertForSequenceClassification.from_pretrained("bert-
base-uncased")
tokenizer = BertTokenizer.from_pretrained("bert-base-
uncased")

# Sample input text for debugging
text = "The weather is beautiful today!"

# Tokenize input text
inputs = tokenizer(text, return_tensors="pt",
padding=True, truncation=True)

# Define the optimizer
```

```python
optimizer = AdamW(model.parameters(), lr=1e-5)

# Move model and inputs to the device
device = torch.device("cuda" if
torch.cuda.is_available() else "cpu")
model.to(device)
inputs = {key: value.to(device) for key, value in
inputs.items()}

# Training loop with debugging features
for epoch in range(5):
    model.train()

    optimizer.zero_grad()

    # Forward pass
    outputs = model(**inputs)
    loss = outputs.loss

    # Check for NaN in loss
    if torch.isnan(loss):
        print("NaN detected in loss, terminating
training.")
        break

    # Backward pass
    loss.backward()

    # Monitor gradients: Check for exploding
gradients
    for name, param in model.named_parameters():
        if param.grad is not None:
            grad_max = param.grad.max().item()
            grad_min = param.grad.min().item()
            print(f"Gradients for {name}:
max={grad_max}, min={grad_min}")

            if grad_max > 1e5:  # Threshold for
exploding gradients
```

```
              print(f"Exploding gradients detected
for {name}, clipping gradients.")

torch.nn.utils.clip_grad_norm_(model.parameters(),
max_norm=1.0)  # Gradient clipping

   optimizer.step()

   # Print loss for every epoch
   print(f"Epoch {epoch+1}, Loss: {loss.item()}")
```

Explanation:
1. **NaN Loss Check**: After the forward pass, we check if the loss is NaN. If it is, we terminate the training loop to prevent further issues.
2. **Gradient Monitoring**: During the backward pass, we monitor the gradients of all parameters. If any gradient exceeds a certain threshold (e.g., 1e5), it indicates **exploding gradients**, and we apply gradient clipping.
3. **Gradient Clipping**: We use **torch.nn.utils.clip_grad_norm_()** to clip gradients and prevent them from becoming too large, which would otherwise cause instability during training.
4. **Loss Monitoring**: The loss is printed at each epoch to track convergence. If the loss becomes unusually large, it could indicate an issue with the model or learning rate.

Expected Output:
During training, the following could be outputted:
- **Gradient Monitoring**: Messages like "Gradients for encoder.layer.0.attention.self.query.weight: max=3.45e+5, min=-2.22e+5", which allow you to spot exploding gradients.
- **Loss Values**: The loss will be printed each epoch, allowing you to track its progress. If NaN values are detected, training will stop.

In this chapter, we explored two important aspects of model training:
1. **Using Captum to Visualize Feature Importance**: We used Captum's **Integrated Gradients** method to visualize how each

token in a sentence influences the model's prediction. This provides insights into the model's decision-making process.

2. **Debugging a Transformer Model's Training Loop**: We implemented strategies for debugging common issues like vanishing gradients, exploding gradients, NaN loss values, and slow convergence. Tools like **gradient clipping**, **loss monitoring**, and **gradient inspection** help ensure that the model trains effectively and stably.

By leveraging these debugging techniques and interpretability tools, you can enhance the training process, gain valuable insights into your model's behavior, and improve model performance in real-world applications

Chapter 13: Ethical and Practical Considerations

The rapid development of Large Language Models (LLMs) has raised a host of **ethical and practical concerns**. As these models increasingly shape our lives, from automating customer service to generating content and assisting with decision-making, it is essential to address the potential risks associated with their deployment. These concerns include issues of **bias**, **data privacy**, **fairness**, and **transparency**. In this chapter, we will explore these critical topics and discuss best practices for the ethical development and deployment of AI systems.

13.1 Identifying and Addressing Bias in LLMs

Overview of Bias in LLMs

Bias in LLMs is a well-documented issue, as these models are often trained on large datasets that reflect existing societal biases. These biases can be related to gender, race, age, ethnicity, or other sensitive attributes, and they can manifest in model predictions and outputs. For example, a language model trained on biased text data might produce outputs that reinforce harmful stereotypes or produce unfair outcomes for certain groups of people.

Sources of Bias:

- **Training Data**: Biases in the training data are one of the primary sources of bias in LLMs. If the data includes biased or unrepresentative content, the model may learn these biases.
- **Model Architecture**: Some aspects of the model's architecture or the way it is trained can amplify biases present in the data.
- **Human Influence**: The design of datasets, the selection of training methods, and even the evaluation process can all introduce bias.

Types of Bias:

1. **Cognitive Bias**: Biases reflecting societal stereotypes, prejudices, or beliefs.

2. **Algorithmic Bias**: Biases that arise from the way algorithms are constructed or optimized.
3. **Historical Bias**: Biases that result from historical injustices and inequalities reflected in the data.

Mitigating Bias in LLMs
There are several strategies to mitigate bias in LLMs:
1. **Dataset Augmentation**: One of the most effective methods is to diversify the training data. By intentionally balancing the representation of various groups or perspectives, we can reduce the model's exposure to biased data.
2. **Fairness Constraints**: Incorporating fairness constraints during training can help ensure that the model's predictions are equitable for all groups.
3. **Post-Processing Techniques**: Techniques like debiasing or fairness-aware prediction can be applied after the model has been trained to adjust biased outputs.

13.2 Data Privacy Concerns in Training Large Language Models

Overview of Data Privacy Concerns
When training LLMs, vast amounts of data are typically used, often collected from the internet, books, and various other sources. Many of these datasets may contain sensitive personal information, raising concerns about data privacy and security. Protecting users' privacy during both the training and deployment phases of LLMs is critical to ensuring that AI systems do not inadvertently harm individuals.

Key Data Privacy Issues:
1. **Personal Data Leakage**: LLMs can memorize and regurgitate parts of the training data, potentially revealing sensitive personal information.
2. **Data Ownership**: Issues around who owns the data used to train models and how that data is shared or monetized.

3. **Regulations**: Compliance with data privacy regulations like **GDPR**, **CCPA**, and other privacy laws that govern the collection, storage, and use of personal data.

Mitigating Privacy Risks:
1. **Differential Privacy**: Using techniques like **Differential Privacy** during training can ensure that the model does not memorize specific data points and reveal them during inference.
2. **Data Anonymization**: Stripping personal identifiers from training datasets ensures that sensitive information is not used.
3. **Secure Data Storage and Access Control**: Ensuring that data is stored securely and access is limited to authorized personnel can help prevent unauthorized data access.

13.3 Ensuring Fairness and Transparency in AI Applications

Overview of Fairness and Transparency
Fairness in AI involves ensuring that the model treats all individuals and groups equally, without discrimination or bias. **Transparency** refers to making AI systems understandable and accountable by providing clear explanations of how decisions are made.

Key Fairness Issues:
1. **Discrimination**: When a model produces biased outputs that disproportionately affect certain groups (e.g., racial or gender bias).
2. **Unequal Impact**: When a model's behavior disproportionately benefits one group while disadvantaging another.

Key Transparency Issues:
1. **Opaque Decision-Making**: AI models, particularly deep learning models like transformers, are often considered "black boxes" because their internal decision-making processes are difficult to interpret.

2. **Lack of Accountability**: Without transparency, it's difficult to understand why a model made a particular decision or who is responsible if something goes wrong.

Ensuring Fairness and Transparency:
1. **Fairness Metrics**: Use fairness metrics (such as **Demographic Parity**, **Equal Opportunity**, etc.) to assess and monitor the fairness of models.
2. **Explainable AI (XAI)**: Employ methods like **LIME** and **SHAP** to interpret model predictions and explain how inputs lead to specific outputs.
3. **Transparent Model Design**: When building and deploying AI systems, ensure that the processes behind the models are documented and accessible.

13.4 Best Practices for Ethical AI Development
Overview of Ethical AI
Building ethical AI systems requires that developers prioritize human rights, fairness, transparency, privacy, and accountability. Ethical AI development isn't just about minimizing harm but also about ensuring that AI systems are beneficial to society.

Key Principles for Ethical AI:
1. **Accountability**: Developers and organizations should be held accountable for the outcomes of the AI systems they create.
2. **Transparency**: The inner workings of AI models should be explainable to users and stakeholders.
3. **Fairness**: AI systems should avoid causing harm to individuals or groups and should work to correct existing biases.
4. **Privacy**: The privacy of users should be protected at all stages of the AI development lifecycle.
5. **Inclusivity**: AI should be developed in a way that benefits all groups, especially marginalized communities.

Best Practices:
1. **Diverse Development Teams**: Encourage diverse perspectives in the development process to reduce unconscious biases and ensure that models are built to serve all groups.
2. **Bias Audits**: Regularly audit models for fairness and bias to ensure they do not perpetuate harmful stereotypes or make discriminatory predictions.
3. **Human-in-the-Loop Systems**: In high-stakes applications, such as healthcare or legal decisions, human oversight should be included to ensure accountability.
4. **Ethical Guidelines**: Establish and follow ethical guidelines and standards for AI development, such as those provided by organizations like **IEEE** or **AI Now Institute**.

Code Example: Mitigating Bias in a Fine-Tuned Model Using Dataset Augmentation

One practical approach to addressing bias in models is **dataset augmentation**. This involves adding diverse examples to the training dataset to ensure that the model is exposed to a more balanced representation of different groups or perspectives. For example, if you are fine-tuning a language model for sentiment analysis, you might augment the dataset to include more diverse sentiment expressions from various cultural contexts.

Code Example: Dataset Augmentation to Mitigate Bias
python

```
from transformers import BertTokenizer,
BertForSequenceClassification, Trainer,
TrainingArguments
from datasets import load_dataset, Dataset
import random

# Load a pre-trained BERT model and tokenizer
model =
BertForSequenceClassification.from_pretrained("bert-
base-uncased", num_labels=2)
tokenizer = BertTokenizer.from_pretrained("bert-base-
uncased")
```

```python
# Load a sample sentiment dataset (positive and
negative reviews)
dataset = load_dataset("imdb")

# Augment dataset with diverse examples (simulating
augmentation for gender and ethnicity fairness)
def augment_data(example):
    augmented_examples = []
    text = example["text"]

    # Simulate adding positive reviews from different
cultural perspectives
    if "good" in text:
        augmented_examples.append({"text": text + "
The reviews are always positive in this community."})
    if "bad" in text:
        augmented_examples.append({"text": text + "
This review has been criticized by different social
groups."})

    return augmented_examples

# Apply augmentation to the training set
augmented_train_data = []
for example in dataset["train"]:
    augmented_train_data.append(example)

augmented_train_data.extend(augment_data(example))

augmented_dataset = Dataset.from_dict({"text":
[x["text"] for x in augmented_train_data]})

# Tokenize the augmented dataset
def tokenize_function(examples):
    return tokenizer(examples["text"],
padding="max_length", truncation=True)
```

```
tokenized_data =
augmented_dataset.map(tokenize_function,
batched=True)

# Define the training arguments
training_args = TrainingArguments(
    output_dir="./results",
    num_train_epochs=3,
    per_device_train_batch_size=8,
    per_device_eval_batch_size=8,
    evaluation_strategy="epoch"
)



# Initialize Trainer
trainer = Trainer(
    model=model,
    args=training_args,
    train_dataset=tokenized_data,
    eval_dataset=tokenized_data
)

# Fine-tune the model with augmented data
trainer.train()
```

Explanation:
1. **Dataset Augmentation**: We augment the training dataset by adding examples that represent diverse perspectives. This can include adding positive reviews from different cultural or demographic contexts to reduce bias towards any specific group.
2. **Fine-Tuning**: The model is fine-tuned on the augmented dataset using the **Trainer** class from Hugging Face, which facilitates efficient model training.

Expected Outcome:
By augmenting the dataset, the model will be trained with a more diverse set of examples, which helps mitigate potential bias in predictions. This ensures the model performs well across different groups and contexts.

In this chapter, we explored several **ethical and practical considerations** that are crucial when developing and deploying LLMs:

1. **Identifying and Addressing Bias**: We discussed the sources of bias in LLMs and explored strategies for mitigating bias through techniques like dataset augmentation.

2. **Data Privacy**: The chapter emphasized the importance of protecting data privacy during the training of LLMs, with suggestions for techniques like **Differential Privacy** and **Data Anonymization**.

3. **Fairness and Transparency**: We examined methods to ensure fairness and transparency in AI applications, highlighting the importance of fairness metrics and explainable AI techniques.

4. **Best Practices for Ethical AI**: We outlined best practices for ensuring ethical AI development, including **bias audits, human-in-the-loop systems**, and the establishment of **ethical guidelines**.

By following these guidelines, AI developers can ensure that their models are not only powerful and efficient but also fair, transparent, and ethically sound, contributing to a more equitable society.

Chapter 14: Case Studies and Emerging Trends

As Large Language Models (LLMs) continue to advance, they are becoming integral to a wide range of applications across different industries. From customer service to healthcare and finance, the potential of LLMs to transform how businesses operate and how services are provided is vast. In this chapter, we will explore:

1. **Success Stories**: Real-world industry-specific applications of LLMs.
2. **Trends in Transformer Architectures**: The emerging advancements in LLMs, such as **Multi-Modal LLMs**, **LLaMA**, and **Falcon**.
3. **PyTorch 2.x**: New features and what the future holds for this popular deep learning framework.

Additionally, we will provide **code examples** on how to implement a **basic multi-modal model** that processes both **text** and **vision** inputs, showcasing the power of combining different data types.

14.1 Success Stories: Industry-Specific Applications of LLMs

LLMs are rapidly being adopted across multiple industries for their ability to process, understand, and generate human-like text. Let's explore some key sectors where LLMs have made a significant impact.

Healthcare: Medical Question Answering and Clinical Decision Support

In healthcare, LLMs have been employed to assist medical professionals by analyzing clinical data, answering medical questions, and providing decision support.

- **Medical Question Answering**: Models like **BioBERT** and **ClinicalBERT** have been fine-tuned on medical literature and patient records, allowing healthcare providers to ask complex questions (e.g., drug interactions, symptom analysis) and receive accurate, evidence-based answers.

- **Clinical Decision Support**: LLMs are used to suggest treatment plans or highlight potential diagnoses based on symptoms, medical history, and test results.

Example Use Case:
- **IBM Watson Health** uses LLMs for decision support in oncology. It analyzes vast amounts of medical literature and patient data to recommend personalized treatment options.

Finance: Automating Risk Assessment and Fraud Detection

In finance, LLMs are being used to automate tasks that would traditionally require human expertise, such as risk assessment, fraud detection, and customer service.

- **Fraud Detection**: LLMs can be trained on historical transaction data to identify unusual patterns that might indicate fraudulent activity.
- **Automated Reporting**: LLMs help financial analysts by generating reports, summarizing market trends, and providing insights into company performance.

Example Use Case:
- **JP Morgan Chase** uses LLMs for contract review and legal document analysis, which speeds up the contract processing time and reduces human error.

Education: Personalized Learning Systems and Tutoring

In education, LLMs are enhancing personalized learning by tailoring educational content to individual students' needs.

- **Personalized Learning**: LLMs analyze students' progress and suggest resources or exercises that match their learning pace and style.
- **Virtual Tutors**: LLM-powered virtual tutors provide real-time assistance to students, answering questions, explaining difficult concepts, and guiding them through exercises.

Example Use Case:
- **Duolingo**, a language-learning app, uses LLMs to provide personalized lessons and practice exercises for users, adapting to their progress and preferred learning methods.

Retail: Customer Support and Product Recommendations

Retailers are using LLMs to enhance customer experience through personalized recommendations, customer service, and automated chatbots.

- **Chatbots and Virtual Assistants**: LLM-powered chatbots handle customer queries, recommend products, and guide users through purchasing decisions.
- **Personalized Recommendations**: By analyzing customer behavior and preferences, LLMs suggest products that are most likely to interest the consumer.

Example Use Case:

- **Amazon** uses LLMs for both product recommendations and to drive its **Alexa** virtual assistant, providing users with a natural, conversational interface for ordering products and controlling smart home devices.

14.2 Trends in Transformer Architectures

As LLMs evolve, new trends in transformer architectures are shaping the future of AI. Let's explore some of the most exciting developments in the field.

Multi-Modal LLMs

Multi-modal LLMs are designed to process multiple types of input data simultaneously, such as text, images, and audio. These models aim to integrate information from various modalities to make more robust and comprehensive predictions.

- **Text + Vision**: Multi-modal models like **CLIP** (Contrastive Language-Image Pre-training) and **DALL·E** are trained to understand both text and images. These models can generate images from textual descriptions and vice versa.
- **Text + Audio**: Models like **Speech-to-Text** and **Text-to-Speech** can combine text and audio inputs for tasks like speech recognition and voice generation.

Emerging Models:
- **OpenAI's CLIP**: A model trained on both images and text, capable of understanding images in the context of textual descriptions. For example, it can match images with the correct textual description even if the image is not explicitly labeled.
- **Google's Flamingo**: A multi-modal model capable of processing both vision and language inputs. It excels at tasks that require both visual context and textual understanding.

LLaMA and Falcon

Two promising architectures that have emerged recently in the LLM space are **LLaMA** and **Falcon**. Both of these models aim to provide highly efficient, high-performing transformers that push the limits of scaling.
- **LLaMA** (Large Language Model Meta AI) is a family of models by Meta that are trained with significantly more efficient architectures compared to previous models like GPT-3. LLaMA provides an efficient and more sustainable approach to scaling LLMs.
- **Falcon**: Developed by the **Technology Innovation Institute (TII)**, Falcon is a new model family that is optimized for more efficient and scalable LLM tasks. It is designed to offer state-of-the-art performance while using fewer resources.

Both **LLaMA** and **Falcon** represent the next wave of advancements in large-scale transformer models, focusing on **performance**, **efficiency**, and **scalability**.

Trends to Watch:
- **Smaller, more efficient LLMs**: A shift toward lightweight, efficient models that perform well even with limited resources.
- **Foundation Models**: More companies are adopting foundational models that can be fine-tuned for specific tasks with less data.

14.3 PyTorch 2.x: Key Features and Future Directions
Overview of PyTorch 2.x

PyTorch has long been a leading deep learning framework, and with the release of **PyTorch 2.x**, several new features have been introduced to improve performance, scalability, and ease of use. PyTorch 2.x focuses on accelerating training and inference, expanding support for distributed computing, and offering better tools for deploying AI models in production.

Key Features in PyTorch 2.x:

1. **TorchDynamo**: A Python-level optimization tool that automatically detects and optimizes certain patterns in the code to improve performance.
2. **AOTAutograd**: This allows for automatic mixed precision training, which improves training efficiency by using both **FP16** and **FP32** data types.
3. **Better Distributed Computing**: PyTorch 2.x enhances the support for multi-node training, including improved scaling and multi-GPU training with distributed backends.

Future Directions:

1. **Model Efficiency**: Continued focus on improving the efficiency of models, making them faster to train, smaller in memory usage, and easier to deploy.
2. **Improved Support for Multi-Modality**: With multi-modal models becoming more important, PyTorch will enhance its support for multi-modal architectures.

Code Example: Implementing a Basic Multi-Modal Model Using Text and Vision Inputs

In this section, we will implement a simple **multi-modal model** that combines **text** and **vision** inputs. Specifically, the model will take both text (e.g., a description) and an image (e.g., a picture) and make predictions based on both data sources.

python

```
import torch
import torch.nn as nn
from transformers import BertModel, BertTokenizer
from torchvision import models, transforms
from PIL import Image
import requests
```

```python
# Load pre-trained models and tokenizer
text_model = BertModel.from_pretrained("bert-base-
uncased")
text_tokenizer = BertTokenizer.from_pretrained("bert-
base-uncased")
vision_model = models.resnet50(pretrained=True)
vision_model.eval()  # Set vision model to evaluation
mode

# Define a multi-modal model combining text and
vision inputs
class MultiModalModel(nn.Module):
    def __init__(self):
        super(MultiModalModel, self).__init__()
        self.text_model = text_model
        self.vision_model = vision_model
        self.fc = nn.Linear(768 + 1000, 2)  # Final
layer for combined output (e.g., binary
classification)

    def forward(self, text_input, image_input):
        # Process text input
        text_output =
self.text_model(**text_input).last_hidden_state[:, 0,
:]  # CLS token output

        # Process image input
        image_output = self.vision_model(image_input)

        # Concatenate text and vision features
        combined_features = torch.cat((text_output,
image_output), dim=1)

        # Output layer
        output = self.fc(combined_features)
        return output

# Instantiate the model
model = MultiModalModel()
```

```
# Example text and image
text = "A beautiful view of the sunset over the
mountains."
image_url = "https://example.com/sunset_image.jpg"  #
Replace with an actual image URL

# Preprocess text
text_input = text_tokenizer(text,
return_tensors="pt", padding=True, truncation=True,
max_length=128)

# Preprocess image
image = Image.open(requests.get(image_url,
stream=True).raw)
transform =
transforms.Compose([transforms.Resize((224, 224)),
transforms.ToTensor(),
transforms.Normalize(mean=[0.485, 0.456, 0.406],
std=[0.229, 0.224, 0.225])])
image_input = transform(image).unsqueeze(0)  # Add
batch dimension

# Make prediction
model.eval()  # Set model to evaluation mode
with torch.no_grad():
    output = model(text_input, image_input)
    print(f"Model output: {output}")
```

Explanation:
1. **Text Model (BERT)**: We use a pre-trained BERT model to process text input. The output from the [CLS] token is used as the text feature representation.
2. **Vision Model (ResNet50)**: We use a pre-trained ResNet50 model to process image input and extract features.
3. **MultiModalModel**: This model combines the text and vision features by concatenating them and passing them through a fully connected layer.
4. **Prediction**: We then pass the concatenated features through the final layer to make predictions (e.g., binary classification).

Expected Outcome:
The model will output a prediction based on both the text and image input. This can be used for tasks like image captioning, visual question answering, or multimodal classification.

In this chapter, we explored some of the most exciting trends and developments in the field of LLMs:

1. **Success Stories**: We discussed how LLMs are being applied across different industries, such as healthcare, finance, education, and retail, to automate processes, improve efficiency, and create personalized experiences.
2. **Trends in Transformer Architectures**: Emerging models like **Multi-Modal LLMs**, **LLaMA**, and **Falcon** are pushing the boundaries of what LLMs can do by integrating multiple data types and improving efficiency.
3. **PyTorch 2.x**: We looked at new features in PyTorch 2.x that improve model performance and distributed computing capabilities.

The **code example** on building a **multi-modal model** demonstrated how to combine text and vision inputs, which is a key trend in AI. By integrating multiple modalities, LLMs are becoming even more powerful and capable of handling a broader range of tasks.

Appendices

A. Installation and Troubleshooting Guide

Setting up PyTorch and Large Language Models (LLMs) can sometimes be challenging, particularly when working with complex dependencies, large models, and multi-GPU setups. In this section, we will cover how to install PyTorch, common installation issues, and troubleshooting strategies.

Installing PyTorch

To install PyTorch, follow these steps based on your environment and preferred installation method.

1. **Installing via pip (for CPU version)**:

bash

pip install torch torchvision torchaudio

This installs PyTorch along with the optional torchvision and torchaudio packages for computer vision and audio processing tasks.

2. **Installing with GPU support (CUDA version)**: PyTorch supports CUDA, enabling it to run efficiently on Nvidia GPUs. To install PyTorch with CUDA support, use the appropriate pip command based on your CUDA version. For example, to install PyTorch with CUDA 11.3 support:

bash

pip install torch==2.0.0+cu113 torchvision==0.13.0+cu113 torchaudio==0.12.0 -f https://download.pytorch.org/whl/torch_stable.html

3. **Verifying the Installation**: After installation, you can verify whether PyTorch was installed correctly by running:

python

```
import torch
print(torch.__version__)  # Check PyTorch version
print(torch.cuda.is_available())  # Check if GPU is available
```

Common Installation Issues

1. **CUDA Version Mismatch**: If PyTorch cannot detect your GPU, it's often due to a CUDA version mismatch between your installed version of PyTorch and the version of CUDA on your machine. Ensure that you install the version of PyTorch that matches your system's CUDA version.

2. **Missing Dependencies**: Some packages, such as torchvision or torchaudio, may require specific system dependencies, such as the C++ compiler or libraries like **libjpeg** or **FFmpeg**. Make sure all dependencies are properly installed.

3. **Permission Issues**: If you encounter permission errors during installation (e.g., "Permission Denied"), try running the installation command with sudo or install it in a virtual environment to avoid system-wide changes.

B. Common PyTorch Commands and Syntax Cheat Sheet

This cheat sheet provides a list of common PyTorch commands and their syntax for reference.

Tensors

- **Create a tensor**:

python

```python
x = torch.tensor([1, 2, 3])  # Create a tensor from a list
x = torch.zeros(3, 3)  # Create a tensor of zeros
x = torch.ones(2, 2)  # Create a tensor of ones
```

- **Tensor Operations**:

python

```python
y = torch.rand(3, 3)
sum_tensor = x + y  # Element-wise addition
diff_tensor = x - y  # Element-wise subtraction
product_tensor = x * y  # Element-wise multiplication
```

- **Reshaping**:

python

```python
x = torch.randn(2, 3)
x_reshaped = x.view(3, 2)  # Reshape the tensor
```

Model Creation
- **Define a simple neural network**:

python

```python
import torch.nn as nn

class SimpleModel(nn.Module):
    def __init__(self):
        super(SimpleModel, self).__init__()
        self.fc1 = nn.Linear(784, 128)
        self.fc2 = nn.Linear(128, 10)

    def forward(self, x):
        x = torch.relu(self.fc1(x))
        x = self.fc2(x)
        return x
```

Training Loop
- **Optimizers and Loss Functions**:

python

```python
model = SimpleModel()
optimizer = torch.optim.SGD(model.parameters(),
lr=0.01)
loss_fn = nn.CrossEntropyLoss()

# Training loop
for epoch in range(10):
    for data, targets in data_loader:
        optimizer.zero_grad()  # Zero the gradients
        outputs = model(data)  # Forward pass
        loss = loss_fn(outputs, targets)  # Compute
loss
        loss.backward()  # Backward pass
        optimizer.step()  # Optimize model
```

C. Glossary of Terms in PyTorch and LLMs

Understanding the terminology in PyTorch and Large Language Models (LLMs) is essential for effectively using these tools. Below is a glossary of key terms.

1. **Tensor**: A multi-dimensional array, similar to NumPy arrays but with additional functionality for GPU acceleration. In PyTorch, tensors are the fundamental data structure for holding data.

2. **Layer**: A single operation in a neural network that processes input and produces output, such as a linear transformation or activation function.

3. **Optimizer**: An algorithm used to adjust model parameters based on the gradients calculated during backpropagation. Common optimizers in PyTorch include **SGD**, **Adam**, and **RMSprop**.

4. **Loss Function**: A function that measures the difference between the model's predictions and the true values. Common loss functions include **Mean Squared Error (MSE)** and **Cross Entropy Loss**.

5. **Backpropagation**: A method for calculating the gradients of the loss function with respect to the model's parameters, allowing the optimizer to adjust the weights during training.

6. **Epoch**: One complete pass through the entire dataset during training.

7. **Overfitting**: When a model learns the training data too well, including noise or outliers, which reduces its ability to generalize to unseen data.

8. **Attention Mechanism**: A component in transformer models that allows the model to weigh the importance of different tokens in the input sequence.

9. **Pre-training and Fine-tuning**: **Pre-training** refers to training a model on a large, general dataset (such as language corpora), and **fine-tuning** involves further training the model on a more specific task or domain dataset.

D. Additional Resources for Learning PyTorch and LLMs

To deepen your knowledge of PyTorch and LLMs, here are some recommended resources:

Books:
1. **"Deep Learning with PyTorch"** by Eli Stevens, Luca Antiga, and Thomas Viehmann – A hands-on guide to PyTorch for deep learning practitioners.
2. **"Transformers for Natural Language Processing"** by Denis Rothman – A comprehensive book on working with transformer-based models, including BERT and GPT.

Online Courses:
1. **Deep Learning Specialization (Coursera)** by Andrew Ng – A foundational series on deep learning, which includes tutorials on PyTorch.
2. **Fast.ai** – Offers a free, practical deep learning course that teaches you to use PyTorch and build state-of-the-art models quickly.

Websites:
1. **PyTorch Documentation**: https://pytorch.org/docs/stable/
2. **Hugging Face**: https://huggingface.co/docs – Provides tutorials and pre-trained models for working with transformers and LLMs.

Communities:
1. **Stack Overflow**: A great place to ask specific PyTorch and LLM-related questions.
2. **PyTorch Forums**: https://discuss.pytorch.org/ – A place to discuss deep learning topics, get help, and contribute to the community.

E. Links to Companion Code Repositories, Colab Notebooks, and Datasets

For hands-on learning, the following resources will help you implement and test the concepts discussed in this book:
1. **Code Repositories**:
   - **PyTorch Examples**: https://github.com/pytorch/examples – Official repository with a variety of deep learning models and examples in PyTorch.
   - **Hugging Face Transformers**: https://github.com/huggingface/transformers – A popular library for working with transformer models like BERT and GPT.

2. **Colab Notebooks**:
   o **Basic PyTorch Tutorial**:
     https://colab.research.google.com/drive/1Z-
     JmHGh1KICbLMKNGI2tV9ZZ_K30xnzT – A beginner-
     friendly PyTorch tutorial notebook.
   o **Fine-Tuning a Transformer Model**:
     https://colab.research.google.com/drive/1e50HpppQ_Lgq
     aLVb7dFZOpnOd3g3ME9B – A notebook to fine-tune
     transformers like BERT on your dataset.
3. **Datasets**:
   o **Hugging Face Datasets**: https://huggingface.co/datasets
     – A large collection of datasets for training and fine-tuning
     LLMs.
   o **Kaggle Datasets**: https://www.kaggle.com/datasets – A
     popular platform for machine learning datasets across
     various domains.
   o **ImageNet**: http://www.image-net.org/ – A large dataset
     for training image classification models.

This book has provided a comprehensive overview of working with
PyTorch and **Large Language Models (LLMs)**. In the appendices, we
covered important installation instructions, common commands and
syntax, a glossary of key terms, additional learning resources, and links
to companion code repositories, Colab notebooks, and datasets. With
this foundation, you're well-equipped to dive into the world of deep
learning and build powerful models for real-world applications.